DISCOVER IN
THE NEW ROBERT'S RULES OF ORDER

- How to use an Internet Relay Chat (IRC) in real time
- The kinds of computer software programs available to help you prepare letters, visual aids, registration packets, and budgets
- How the World Wide Web can help you gather information you need for that important meeting

The New Robert's Rules of Order, second edition, offers these ideas and many more. Easy to understand and completely up-to-the-minute, it is an essential reference that will help carry your organization into the new millennium.

THE IDEAL REFERENCE FOR CLUBS,
CHURCHES, CIVIC GROUPS, AND OTHER
ORGANIZATIONS LARGE OR SMALL
THAT CONDUCT FORMAL MEETINGS

MARY A. DE VRIES has arranged and conducted hundreds of meetings of all sizes, participating in all aspects of meeting activity from budgeting to registration. A specialist in communication and word usage, she is the author of 50 books, including *How to Run a Meeting* (Plume) and two other Signet titles: *The Practical Writer's Guide* and *The New American Handbook of Letter Writing.*

THE NEW
ROBERT'S
RULES OF
ORDER

Second Revised Edition

Mary A. De Vries

A SIGNET BOOK

SIGNET
Published by the Penguin Group
Penguin Putnam Inc., 375 Hudson Street,
New York, New York 10014, U.S.A.
Penguin Books Ltd, 27 Wrights Lane,
London W8 5TZ, England
Penguin Books Australia Ltd, Ringwood,
Victoria, Australia
Penguin Books Canada Ltd, 10 Alcorn Avenue,
Toronto, Ontario, Canada M4V 3B2
Penguin Books (N.Z.) Ltd, 182–190 Wairau Road,
Auckland 10, New Zealand

Penguin Books Ltd, Registered Offices:
Harmondsworth, Middlesex, England

First published by Signet, an imprint of Dutton NAL,
a member of Penguin Putnam Inc.

First Printing, January, 1990
First Printing (Second Revised Edition), May, 1998

10 9 8 7 6 5 4 3 2 1

CONTENTS

MEETING CONDUCT:
THE NEW ROBERT'S RULES OF ORDER

Contents

Contents

PREFACE

This second edition of *The New Robert's Rules of Order* has been extensively revised with two objectives in mind: to bring the first part of the book about meeting arrangements into the electronic age and to clarify and simplify further the complex rules in the second part of the book about meeting conduct. As nearly a decade has passed since the first edition was published, pursuing those objectives involved making some significant changes in this edition.

Because meeting arrangements logically precede meeting conduct, the material on arrangements also precedes the rules about conduct in this edition. To make the arrangements material current, however, we not only updated and reorganized the existing chapters but also added two new chapters—an introductory chapter on understanding meetings (Chapter 1) and a chapter about the electronic technologies that have reshaped meetings of all types and sizes in the modern world (Chapter 2).

In Chapter 1, you'll find new material about different types of meetings and the special concerns of meeting planners in setting up an international meeting or a meeting with foreign participants. This chapter also includes a new list of tips on handling a stressful meeting, a matter of special concern to attendees as well as arrangers.

In Chapter 2, you'll notice that the new technologies have made many more choices, such as desktop computer conferencing, available to meeting arrangers. Even when a conventional, rather than an electronic, meeting is desired, the various tasks required to make the arrangements have been simplified by the new technologies. The computer, for example, is now used for everything from preparing and transmitting meeting notices to preparing and filing the meeting minutes.

The rest of the chapters in the first part of the book describe common activities in planning and organizing a meeting and in handling the other key aspects of meeting arrangements. In setting up a large meeting, these activities often include arrangements for finances, program development, publicity and promotion, registration, facilities, and common types of meeting records.

As the title, *The New Robert's Rules of Order,* indicates, however, the main focus of this revised edition, like that of the previous edition, is on the *conduct* of meetings. The second part of the book, therefore, consists of the full 1893 work of the famous *Robert's Rules of Order,* by General H. M. Robert, rewritten in simple, easy-to-follow, contemporary English.

The fact that General Robert's 1893 text (an update of his original 1876 text) has survived so long attests to its value and enduring importance. Thus, we have not changed the rules that General Robert developed, although an organization that wants to modify any of his 1893 rules may do so to suit its own needs.

What is different about *The New Robert's Rules of Order* is the language used to present and explain General Robert's 1893 text. Our first edition took a large step toward modernizing the archaic language and simplifying the complex and cumbersome explanations of the rules. This revised edition takes a further step in that direction in keeping with the more relaxed style of putting the original rules into practice today.

In this revised edition, we again decided to keep General Robert's exact order of topics and his numbering of the sections. Response to our first edition clearly indicated that many readers, who are by now familiar with the arrangement of topics in the 1893 text, don't want to have to learn a new organizational plan. So if you're used to remembering and referring to the original rules by number, or if you're discussing the rules with someone who also uses General Robert's original order of topics, you need not learn any new numbers or search through a different order of topics.

A quick-reference table of rules about motions is given at the end of this book—just before the main index—so that you can turn to it immediately, without searching. Whether you're a participant in, or the chair of, a meeting, you may need to check a point *quickly* during a meeting. The table of rules is designed to answer up to two hundred questions about parliamentary practice. For a detailed description of the parliamentary rules, refer to the introduction to the second part of this book—"Meeting Conduct: The New Robert's Rules of Order."

While preparing this revised edition of *The New Robert's Rules of Order,* I again benefited from the suggestions and advice of parliamentary expert and consultant Jean McCormack. In addition to providing parliamentary counsel, she has arranged and conducted numerous meetings and has been active in various committees in both business and social organizations of various types and sizes. I greatly appreciated her invaluable contribution to this revised edition.

HOW TO USE THIS WORK

The first part of the book—"Meeting Arrangements: Practices and Procedures"—is straightforward; to find topics you can simply look at the table of contents or check the general subject index at the end of the book. The second part—"Meeting Conduct: The New Robert's Rules of Order"—is much more complex. If you follow these steps, however, you should soon become an expert in using the rules of order in actual meetings:

- Review the table of contents for Parts I, II, and III (based on the 1893 edition) carefully and try to fix in your mind the articles in each part. In Part I, for instance, Article I is "Introduction to Business"; Article II is "General Classification of Motions"; and so forth.

- After studying the article titles in the table of contents, reread them once more and glance below each one at the related sections to gain a general impression of the type of material in that portion of the text (but don't try to memorize the section titles). For example, under Article XII, "Motions," you'll see that there are eight sections (nos. 55–63). According to the titles, the text of these sections will tell you things such as how to modify or amend a motion, how to defer action, how to suppress debate, or how to suppress a question.

- Now that you have a good idea of what the three parts contain—from reading the article and section titles—read the introduction to the part of the book devoted to the rules of order. It will give a thumbnail definition of parliamentary law and describe the plan of the work (as shown in the table of contents).

- Next, turn to the end of the book, to the "Quick-Reference Guide to Motions," where you'll find all of the motions summarized in a table of rules, along with a list of the precedence of motions and the forms (the wording) of putting certain questions to a vote. This quick-reference material is what you'll use when you're in the midst of a meeting and don't have time to search the main text for answers. But don't try to memorize the table and lists just yet; simply look at them so that you'll know generally what is there.

- Now go back to the beginning of the text ("Part I. Rules of Order") and page through the entire text of the rules, glancing at each page only long enough to learn how much discussion is available for each topic. Then as soon as you have time, read the entire text slowly and carefully. Read the quick-reference section at the end of the book, which should be much easier to use and understand after having read the preceding text discussions.

Assuming you have followed the above steps and are at least more familiar now with parliamentary practice than you were before, you are ready to test your knowledge in an actual meeting as either an attendee, an officer, or the chair of the group. Either way, keep the book at your side and follow these steps when a question arises:

- Check the table at the end of the book—just before the general index—to see which rules apply to which motions.

- Check the precedence-of-motions list in the quick-reference section when you need to determine the rank (higher or lower) of motions (that is, which motions comes first).

- Check the quick-reference section examples of forms of putting certain questions to a vote when you want to know the proper wording of a particular question.

- If the quick-reference material doesn't solve your problem, look up the subject in the general index at the end of the book or look in the table of contents and then turn to the applicable article or section in the text in which more details are given.

If after doing all of the above you still feel overwhelmed by the details of parliamentary practice; take heart: The more you use the book—and the various indexes and quick-reference tools built into it—the easier it will become and the more you'll appreciate the fact that the rules of order are meant to be used not only by officers of important assemblies but by everyone in any type of meeting of any size.

MEETING ARRANGEMENTS: PRACTICES AND PROCEDURES

1. UNDERSTANDING MEETINGS

The Meeting Paradox

Meetings are one of the few things in life that are pursued relentlessly even though they provoke endless complaints of frustration, stress, wasted hours, and dissatisfaction with the outcome. Why is something that is so often annoying and unsatisfactory staunchly supported as essential to decision making and the conduct of business? No doubt it's because meetings are just that—essential to decision making and the conduct of business.

The majority of people in clubs, associations, businesses, and other organizations are unwilling or unable to make unilateral decisions and take unilateral action on behalf of others. Either the organization's rules won't permit it, or the desire to build consensus and gain the support of others prevails. The result is a call for a meeting, one that probably will follow closely on the heels of a previous meeting and may end barely in time for the participants to prepare for the next one.

Meeting Management

A meeting-weary businessperson once listed meetings as one of the three absolutes in life: death, taxes, and meetings. One way to make a constant factor such as this more acceptable—even enjoyable—is to manage it better. Those who want to control the influence of meetings on their lives are usually eager to accept ideas and strategies for managing meetings more effectively. A necessary ingredient in reaching that goal is knowledge—understanding how meetings work and what types of practices and procedures are followed in arranging successful meetings.

This first part of the book describes the common pre-meeting tasks that must be managed carefully to ensure a successful event. The second part is a parliamentary guide to conducting meetings based on the widely accepted rules of order created by General H. M. Robert.

Types of Meetings

An informal meeting of a few people, such as the executive committee meeting of a condo association or the staff meeting of an executive and his or her office assistants, can be arranged quickly and easily. Usually, all that is needed is a few telephone calls suggesting a time to meet and a place to hold the meeting, such as in someone's house or office or in a restaurant or other suitable place.

Arranging a formal meeting of larger groups, however, involves many more steps. Often the group has official rules that must be followed in regard to the meeting notice, time and place of the meeting, who may attend and vote, and other matters.

With the increasing opportunities made available by computers, questions about the type of meeting to hold have become especially important. The next chapter, therefore, considers electronic technologies that are having a strong impact on the way in which people meet and how they exchange information. For example, will people gather in the same room to talk to one another? Or will they contact one another from different remote locations through computers or video broadcast equipment?

Common Meetings. Organizations must consider a variety of factors in deciding what type of meeting to schedule—expected attendance, location, purpose, and audience. In addition, organizations must decide whether they want a *conventional meeting,* such as a board of directors' meeting, conducted by a presiding officer, or whether they want another type of meeting.

Instead of a conventional meeting, an organization may want to have an open-space, *round-table meeting.* This type of meeting has no tables, just chairs arranged in a circle. It also has no agendas. The participants—not the presiding officer—decide what to discuss.

Perhaps a *focus group* is needed. This type of meeting, dealing with a particular topic or concern, may consist of a small, randomly selected but representative group of consumers who are questioned about their views on a new product or service.

If an emergency has occurred, an *ad hoc meeting* may be necessary to deal with the situation. This type of meeting is called for a specific purpose. In an emergency, it is called on short notice and is held for as long as necessary to end the crisis or solve the problem.

Or an entirely different type of meeting may be desired, one that takes advantage of the new electronic technologies described in the next chapter. Business associates in different field offices may want to work together on a business report but may be unable to travel to a particular site. Therefore, they may decide to hold a *document conference* in which the participants in their different locations communicate through their computers, which are interlinked by the telephone lines and the network to which they all belong. Networks and various forms of electronic conferencing are described in the next chapter.

Sometimes a large conference or convention is required. Businesses may need the format of booths and exhibits to market their equipment or merchandise. Or an association may hold a large information conference for both members and nonmembers. Usually, all meetings of this magnitude run over a period of at least several days.

It's clear that one can arrange almost any type of meeting that the participants want to hold. Therefore, two or three people may meet in someone's office to discuss activity for the day, twenty people may gather in a corporate conference room to view an advertising presentation, thirty-five people may attend a data-processing seminar in another city, or two thousand people may travel to the annual conference of a technical society.

The preceding examples suggest that a good way to categorize meetings is by size, from a one-on-one office meeting to a convention with thousands of attendees. Size is important because it directly affects the organizational requirements for a meeting—site, costs, duration, and so on. But there are also other useful classifications for meetings, such as degree of formality, principal activity, frequency of occurrence, or main objective.

To some, the most critical factor is not the method of classification but whether the meeting is truly legitimate or necessary. Most legitimate meetings are arranged to make a decision, solve a problem, exchange information, develop new ideas ("brainstorm"), work on a project or document, transact business, or conduct a ceremonial function. A meeting that someone calls simply for self-aggrandizement, such as to hear himself or herself talk or to blame others for his or her bad decisions, is soon exposed as unnecessary or irresponsible.

The International Meeting. Meetings in the United States or in other countries with foreign participants pose special problems. For businesspeople, the success of such meetings may be crucial to the success of a proposed venture or new trade arrangement. Therefore, it's essential that the organizers take steps to avoid an unfortunate faux pas that could offend the foreign guests and destroy opportunities for good business relations. Those who want to host or attend international meetings should consider various key questions in advance, for example:

- Have you thoroughly studied the background of the foreign participants?

- Is the language being used in conversations, discussions, presentations, and so on free of clichés, idioms, and other expressions that would be confusing to a foreign visitor?

- Would the flip charts, color slides, and other presentations be considered too gaudy and elaborate for the foreign participants?

- Do the foreign visitors need more basic information and more detailed explanations than U.S. attendees require?

- Will the foreign visitors consider it inappropriate to conclude a final agreement at the meeting?

- Will you or the foreign visitors require on-site interpreters and a translation of the written minutes or proceedings?

- Which foods and beverages might be taboo to a foreign guest?

- Which hand, facial, and other body gestures—although common and appropriate in the United States—are considered offensive in the foreign visitor's country?

- How much informality, if any, is acceptable in the other country?

- Have you made arrangements for appropriate hotels and transportation for the foreign guests?

- Have one or more people been assigned to assist the foreign participants—and their spouses—during their stay in the United States?

The Stressful Meeting. No one plans on a stressful meeting. Sometimes it just happens, but more often it occurs when poor planning or other factors lead to a stressful atmosphere. For example, a stressful meeting may occur when attendees are hungry or tired, when the topics under consideration cause strong disagreement, when some members are unruly, or when the presiding officer loses control of the schedule, the agenda, or something else. Here are a few examples of common stress-reducing strategies:

- Lead by example in matters of courtesy and respect for others, regardless of their views.

- Have firm ground rules about interruptions, disruptive behavior, filibustering, and so on.

- Schedule refreshment breaks between main meals to ward off fatigue and resulting attention loss or irritability.

- Do your homework in advance to avoid making others wait while you do on-the-spot research.

- Watch for signs of tension and, if necessary, postpone an explosive matter until a more favorable time.

- Arrange for the use of ergonomic equipment and furniture to lessen physical and mental strain.

- Use humor and anecdotes effectively to relieve stressful moments.

- Consider whether two or more shorter meetings would be less exhausting than a single, overly long meeting.

What's Ahead

The following chapters look at the practices and procedures followed in arranging legitimate semiformal and formal meetings. In addition to summarizing important new electronic meeting technologies, this part of the book describes traditional steps in organizing and planning an event—from setting objectives to signing up speakers, publicizing the event, contacting prospective participants, selecting the site, arranging for the meeting facilities, and preparing the permanent meeting records.

2. ELECTRONIC MEETING TECHNOLOGIES

The Impact of Electronic Technologies

The word *meeting* formerly referred only to a gathering of people with common interests, all appearing in person at the same physical location or meeting site. Not so today. Electronic, or computer, technology has caused the traditional definition to become much broader.

People in different locations can now meet by using telephone and cable-television lines, radio waves, or satellites that are capable of carrying data, graphics, voice signals, and video images over long distances. Even if the technical details and inner workings of modern transmission or broadcast technology are a mystery, anyone who watches television or makes long-distance telephone calls understands the results.

Whether or not everyone attending a meeting is well informed technologically, the common electronic technologies, such as fax transmission and computer document preparation, are having a strong impact on meetings in groups of all sizes. Even a small, local garden club may use a computer to prepare its monthly program bulletin and to type its meeting notices. In larger organizations, the use of a variety of electronic technologies, from computer-scheduling programs to large-scale video transmission, is widespread and firmly established.

However, the opportunities opened up by electronic technologies haven't always made life simpler or easier. For example, the everyday use of the computer in both small- and large-group communications hasn't caused the number of meetings held by a club or other organization to decrease. To the contrary, organizations are holding more meetings each year, are holding them more often, and are holding meetings that run slightly longer than they did in the past.

The positive changes caused by electronic technologies have occurred primarily in meeting *practices*. Two familiar changes of this type are the sharp reduction of manual tasks associated with making meeting arrangements and the greater possibilities for instant long-distant contacts without the need for physical travel.

The Computer

With home computers becoming as commonplace as television sets and VCRs, most households now have at least one member who is familiar with computer communications. The use of computers in business is even more prevalent. For example, businesses of all types and sizes now routinely require that applicants for office positions must have good computer skills. Many of the meeting arrangements described in the following pages are therefore handled by computer in both small groups and large organizations.

Members of small groups use desktop personal computers (PCs) or smaller, portable notebook computers to handle everything from preparing meeting agendas to setting up and filing meeting minutes. The PCs and notebook computers used for such tasks are typically small, stand-alone machines with, at a minimum, the following components:

- A central processing unit (the brains of the computer)

- A monitor, with a televisionlike display screen

- A keyboard, which resembles a typewriter keyboard but, additionally, has numerical keys and other special-use keys

- A printer, which prints pages of the material that users key (type) into their machines and view on the display screens of their monitors

Some users enlarge their systems to include various other devices. A *modem,* for example, may be added to connect a computer to a telephone. It then converts the material prepared by the computer into a form that will travel over the telephone lines to another receiving computer that also includes a modem.

Computer Software. With the appropriate *software*— a program installed in a computer to enable it to perform certain tasks—users can handle many meeting functions with ease. For example:

- With a *word processing program,* you can prepare agendas, meeting notices, minutes, and other material and type, correct, and print or file (store electronically) the material.

- With *accounting or spreadsheet programs,* you can keep accounting records, prepare budgets and various financial statements, prepare income tax returns, and generally handle the overall financial record-keeping needs of a group.

- With *scheduling and planning programs,* you can organize and plan meetings of all sizes and maintain a calendar for an entire year or longer.

- With a *desktop-publishing program,* you can prepare sophisticated conference programs, registration packets, and large books of conference speeches (proceedings).

- With a *graphics program,* you can prepare visual aids, diagrams, and other artwork, such as the floorplan of booths for convention exhibits.

- With an *E-mail program,* you can prepare letters, memos, and other messages and send them to—or receive correspondence from—other network users who also have units equipped for E-mail.

A program exists for nearly every major task associated with a meeting and can be used to handle the basic meeting arrangements described in the following chapters.

The Fax Machine. Fax machines may be individual units apart from a computer or may be integrated with a computer. When a separate fax machine is used, you have to prepare the message or document to be sent by computer or other means, print a copy, and physically take it to the stand-alone fax unit for transmission. When fax and computer capabilities are integrated and a modem connects the combined unit to the telephone, you can both prepare and send a message from the same machine.

Although not every home has a fax machine, people who want to send faxes can use commercial fax services. Certain stores, mail services, and other establishments will send or receive a letter or other document for a small fee.

Electronic Networks

In businesses, individual desktop computer units may be wired to one another to form a small network of interconnected units. When the various computer terminals in a business are physically wired together, the resulting network is called a *local-area network* (*LAN*).

Sometimes the computers are each connected to a single large central computer. This large unit contains the processing capability (brains) for all of the individual workstation units, or terminals, that are connected to it. In addition, the individual units may be all connected to a single, large-capacity, high-speed printer.

When each individual workstation consists of only a keyboard and a monitor, it can't function fully without the aid of the large central computer and the large-capacity printer. This type of incomplete, or dependent, terminal is commonly called a *dumb terminal.*

Individual computer units that are connected in a network have built-in modems or separate devices linking the computers to the telephone lines. With this type of connection, users in remote locations can then dial up one another to communicate electronically. The information that is sent or received can be viewed on the user's monitor or printed in paper (hard-copy) form on the user's printer.

The Internet. The largest of all electronic networks is the *Internet.* It is actually a huge network of networks, consisting of numerous other interconnected smaller networks and millions of computer users worldwide. The electronic road map that enables Internet users to reach different places, businesses, or people (sites) is called the *World Wide Web* (*WWW* or *the Web*).

The Web is so named because it has many sites linked together as in a spider web. Web users can best move from one such site to another by installing in their computers a "navigation" type of computer program. Such a program has instructions for moving around the Web and finding desired information.

People as well as businesses can do more than move from one established Web site to another. They can set up their own site with their own information, called a *home page.* They can then establish an *electronic address* so that other Internet users will be able to locate their home pages. Electronic addresses, in fact, are also necessary for users to send and receive electronic-mail (E-mail) messages on any network.

Access to the Internet is available by subscription through local Internet service providers (see your Yellow Pages). These service providers will supply instructions for using the Internet through their systems. Instructions for using other individual networks, such as CompuServe, American Online, or Prodigy, which offer additional services, are provided by the individual organization.

Electronic Conferencing

Once the purview of business, electronic meetings are now within the reach of individuals who each have a computer, modem, telephone, and access to a network. *Internet Relay Chat* (*IRC*), for example, is a multiuser Internet program that allows users worldwide to "meet" on the screens of their computer monitors to discuss specific subjects with one another. You can pick from dozens of subjects (channels) and meet electronically with others on the same channel to discuss the chosen topic.

After following the instructions to make the appropriate Internet connection and then following the instructions given on your computer screen for using the IRC, you are ready to meet and converse electronically. You need only type a comment and press *Enter* on your keyboard to have that comment seen by everyone else that has chosen the same IRC channel. Since these electronic discussions, or exchanges, take place immediately, the exchange is said to be in *real time*.

The real-time aspect of the IRC is in contrast to an E-mail type of *forward-and-store exchange*. In that case, a message sent by one computer user to another on the same network is stored at the destination until the receiver is ready to retrieve it and respond to it.

Business users, like private individuals, may exchange electronic messages in real time by using a computer, modem, the telephone lines, and the required access procedures for their networks. But electronic meetings in the business world are often much more complex than a simple Internet discussion or exchange of E-mail messages.

The Teleconference. A *teleconference* is another name for an electronic conference—a meeting of people in two or more locations that is usually handled with electronic equipment. Whereas a simple long-distance conference call may involve no more than a telephone connection between two people, a full-scale videoconference may involve small groups of people in different locations who converse by television-style broadcasting. The more elaborate types of teleconferences can be set up by working with a local telephone company and vendors who rent specially equipped rooms with lighting, sound, and video equipment.

Although sound and images may be sent between locations by radio waves or satellites, telephone lines are involved in most long-distance electronic meeting exchanges. The newer but less-common *wide-band telephone lines* offer faster speeds than the conventional lines used in traditional voice communication. The wide band most often used for conferencing, where available, is the Integrated Services Digital Network (ISDN).

The following are some of the principal types of teleconferences being conducted by organizations of all sizes:

- A basic *audioconference* is a simple telephone conference call. Two or more participants can hear but cannot see one another. When the telephone conference takes place through the use of a *full-duplex audio system,* voice signals can be sent in both directions between sender and receiver at the same time. When a *half-duplex system* is used, signals can be sent both ways, but only one way at a time

- An *audiographic conference* is an audioconference with the additional use of fax equipment. Participants in different locations talk to one another on the telephone in the usual manner, and they also exchange paper documents by faxing them back and forth.

- A *speakerphone audioconference* is another variation of the conventional telephone conference. By adding loudspeaker devices and microphones to a telephone, several people in the same room can listen to people in another location without each person needing his or her own telephone receiver.

- A basic *computer* (or *document or data-sharing*) *conference* is an exchange of data between computer network users in two or more locations. Participants, who interlink their computers by way of a modem and the telephone lines, can simultaneously view the same document on their computer screens and can work together on the document, all at the same time.

- An *audio computer conference* (or *voice-data conference*) is a variation of the basic computer conference in which participants all work together on the same document. In this type of meeting, participants in the different locations additionally use headsets so that they can talk with one another while their hands remain free to use on their keyboards.

- A *desktop videoconference* is a more complex form of the basic audio computer conference. In this case, participants additionally have special videoconferencing programs installed in their computers and a tiny camera attached to their monitors. They can thus hear and see one another on their computer screens while they are working on a document. However, the image of each person usually occupies only a small portion of the screen

- A *full-motion videoconference* is another type of meeting in which participants in different locations can see one another on their computer screens. This type of meeting may take place in a room especially equipped for video and computer transmissions, or it may involve only a small, specially equipped portable cart that can be rolled to the desired room. With advanced full-motion video, images are provided at a resolution close to that of VHS videotape used in VCRs. Shots of the participants appear on the full area of the computer screen.

- A *large-audience videoconference,* or *interactive broadcasting,* is most common among Fortune 500 companies. This type of system is capable of providing a video and audio exchange between large groups (more than fifty people) in different locations. Specially equipped rooms have large storage sets, props, broadcast-quality cameras, special sound and lighting equipment, computers, fax machines, visual-aid equipment, and other special equipment, such as copy boards for making and transmitting instant copies of presentations and other material. Also provided are trained technicians, directors, and other staff experienced in commercial television broadcasting.

Any form of conferencing that involves expensive equipment and trained personnel is financially and technically beyond the capability of most organizations. Although some large corporations have their own in-house video broadcast facilities, most that want to conduct a large-scale videoconference rent the required facilities, equipment, and technical staff.

Meeting arrangements for a sophisticated electronic

conference involve extensive cooperation with many outside providers. For example, the meeting arrangements will include working with the vendors who rent, set up, and run the equipment, as well as with the telephone company or other organization that provides transmission cables, satellite links, or other means of transmission or broadcast.

Whether a meeting is conducted by computer over long distances or conventionally by participants meeting in person in the same location, certain basic arrangements are necessary. The following chapters describe the major requirements in arranging a semiformal or formal meeting, such as a conference or convention.

3. ORGANIZATION AND PLANNING

Meeting Objectives

Need for a Meeting. Is a meeting really necessary? It can be difficult to define the objectives of a meeting if it isn't even necessary to have one. All too often this is the case. One gets the impression that people often meet merely out of habit and that they have lost the ability to act alone or through less time-consuming means.

You may remember from your school science lessons that certain species appear to have lost abilities or attributes they used to have. Some fish living forever in deep, dark waters have lost their need for eyes and have become sightless. Some land creatures formerly with wings have stopped flying and have become earthbound.

Have we lost our ability to function without a meeting? No doubt you can document cases of unnecessary meetings. Yet this shouldn't cloud the fact that without person-to-person contact at work and in social settings, and without organized assemblies of people who have common needs and interests, a substantial amount of activity would come to a halt, and important needs would remain unattended.

The Objectives. Some of the basic factual questions—about time and place, for example—are easier to answer than more intellectually challenging questions, such as those dealing with concepts or objectives. Meeting planners, therefore, often fail to deal adequately with the really tough questions, such as the big one: how to define the meeting objectives.

Many meetings, such as staff, committee, or board meetings, may have multiple objectives. They may, for example, want to present or exchange information, to solve a problem, to make a decision, to plan an event, to make work assignments, and to investigate a problem. Yet the various objectives may not be equally important. A board of directors, for instance, may meet primarily to nominate new officers, but it may also want to take care of several other secondary matters before adjourning.

Variations in Objectives. The reasons for meeting vary with the type of business or professional activity of the participants. A parent-teacher association is involved in activities that are very different from those of a computer manufacturer's sales team. The parent-teacher association may meet to discuss student events and a changing educational curriculum in response to its concern with educational goals and needs. The sales team, however, may be motivated strictly by profit and may meet to plot sales strategy or prepare to introduce a new product to consumers.

Each organization may also have vastly different objectives from one meeting to another. A church body on one occasion may hold a meeting to determine whether a member who violated some rules should be expelled. On another occasion, it may be concerned with its annual budget. A hospital committee or board may meet on one or more occasions to plan the addition of a new wing. On another occasion, it may want to discuss new operating-room procedures.

In some cases, different people attend each meeting. A hospital board of directors may meet with members of a planning committee to discuss adding a new wing. At the same time, an operating-room staff may go out of town to attend a seminar with other personnel from other hospitals to learn about new operating-room procedures.

Because the subject of meetings is so broad, the first part of this book is only a brief overview of important steps to take in arranging a meeting. Each organization and each meeting will have its own unique requirements, and those responsible for the arrangements must tailor procedures to fit their particular situations.

The Master Plan

An important point to remember in planning and organizing a meeting is that planning should precede action. Whether you're working alone or are part of a planning committee, where do you start? Gathering information is an excellent way to start the planning steps. Collect as many details about the prospective meeting as possible and set up paper or computer information files right away.

If you don't know where to begin, however, take a pencil and paper or sit down at your computer. Imagine that you're a student ready to prepare a class assignment. Your assignment in this case is to devise a meeting blueprint or master plan. Furthermore, assume that the meeting will be much more than a simple two-person office conference or social exchange. Perhaps it will be an out-of-town seminar or something else with at least one room full of participants.

If your computer has a planning or scheduling program, the task of devising a master meeting plan may be much easier. Simply call up the program on your computer screen and follow its instructions.

In any case, to prepare a detailed master plan, you need to identify everything that will go in the plan: a general manager and a meeting coordinator, a proposed meeting chair, committees to handle the various aspects of the meeting (finance, program, site and facilities, exhibits, audiovisual and other equipment, meals and refreshments, entertainment, registration, publicity, mailings, proceedings publication, and so forth), administrative and clerical staff to process information, guest speakers, and anything else that applies to the meeting. The larger and more complex the meeting, the more things you will need to include.

Your master plan needs something else: *evaluation or analysis*—before, during, and after the meeting. For this, you'll want to identify key individuals with whom you'll brainstorm. List some matters you'll want to discuss with them, for example:

- A written statement of the need for and purpose of the meeting

- A theme or title (for a conference, seminar, or other large meeting)

- An estimate of support from interested persons

- Alternative plans if the master design needs revision later

- Strategies for motivating people, collecting data, controlling schedules, monitoring progress, and evaluating success at each stage of operations

- Procedures (how will the functions be handled, how will finances be controlled, and so on?)

The participants at the meeting probably won't be aware of your preliminary work. All of the things they see and receive at the meeting will not appear out of the ordinary, but you'll know that they didn't just happen with the snap of your fingers. You'll also know that the meeting might have been a disaster if you hadn't had a good master plan and the necessary controls to guide you—with backup strategies and alternative steps to take should anything suddenly go wrong.

Initial Outline. The final version of your master plan may be very different from your initial effort. But for now, you need to prepare at least an outline so that the discussion at your first organization and planning meeting won't wander aimlessly.

If you're planning a small, uncomplicated meeting, however, there may be no key individuals to form a planning committee. You may be a committee of one. In that case, you will need a detailed plan even more— to be certain that you can maintain control over the numerous planning and organizing details that must be handled.

Even on your initial outline, make an effort to describe the type of meeting you visualize—including aspects that are already decided (it *has* to be a sales meeting) and those that are open to suggestions (*where* you'll hold the meeting). Or list first, second, and third choices to present at the initial planning and organizing meeting.

Identifying the kind of meeting it will be is the easy part. Will it be a sales meeting? A chapter meeting of your professional association? A training workshop for your departmental staff? Something else? The purpose also should be clear. Will the purpose be to learn something? To exchange information? To solve some problem at work? To accomplish something else?

In regard to site and related matters, however, more thought and decision making will be involved. Will it be necessary to meet locally? To hold an electronic meeting, such as a videoconference? To arrange a two-day meeting in a hotel out of town, with meals, transportation, and so forth provided?

Your final plan will have open slots in it for the place and date and, eventually, for the times when speeches, discussions, meals, and so on are scheduled. All that you can do now, however, is list alternatives.

If you will be meeting away from your office, you will need to select the site and find out if reservations can be made for the dates and times you prefer. After evaluating the estimated attendance, costs, and convenience of various sites in terms of travel and time away from work, you may need to modify your initial thoughts about location.

All this information is tentative, like many other details. Nevertheless, you want to mention everything imaginable now, knowing that more complete facts will be filled in later.

After you've outlined the principal areas you need to consider *in advance*—before anyone, staff or other, goes to work on arrangements—you can start to add details. Depending on what you have in mind for a meeting, some of the things previously listed on your initial outline may not apply, or there may be other considerations that you'll want to include.

Record Keeping

Meeting Forms. Depending on the complexity of your proposed meeting, you may or may not need formal scheduling, budget, and other forms. However, most organizations already have or will secure standard forms, such as a budget-authorization form or an equipment checklist, to use in making the meeting arrangements. (The checklist is used to check off each overhead projector, microphone, and so on as it arrives and as it is set up in the meeting room.)

You may also have a planning and scheduling computer program. For example, there may be a computerized annual meeting calendar or schedule that you have to check for open slots and then record your meeting date on one of the open slots. If your organization holds multiple meetings each year, you may be required (or want) to schedule all of your meetings in advance for the entire year.

If your company doesn't have computer forms or printed meeting forms, inquire at an office-supply store for standard forms. Or if you have scanning equipment to transfer already-prepared material into your computer, order a copy of a conference-planning book that has sample forms you can use. Your local library may have such books, and most well-stocked bookstores that handle business-related subjects carry them.

For a large conference or convention, planning forms and checklists are a must. Even for a small meeting, a simplified version of such material is invaluable to the person who has to keep track of numerous details and supervise assistants who are handling some of the arrangements.

The larger the meeting, the more formal your records must be. But anything is better than nothing. Even a simple to-do checklist is invaluable. In addition, you can create various other lists, such as a staff-assignment checklist: meals—Roy; room reservations—Jody; and so on.

Files. Although you may be skilled at filing ideas in your mind, it's not a good idea to rely on your memory even with simple office meetings. To be certain that you don't forget something, spell out your ideas and file them in your electronic and paper files.

Having specific information available on your computer or in paper form will be helpful not only to you but to others. In case you become ill or have another emergency that makes it impossible for you to continue work on the arrangements, others need to have something in writing that explains what has already been done and what still needs to be done.

Task Assignments

As soon as you have at least a skeletal plan in mind, it's time to meet with key individuals (if any) and form committees or, in the case of a small meeting, make task assignments for your staff. How all of this is handled depends on your organization's usual policy.

Some permanent organizations require that committee appointments and similar assignments be handled at an organized assembly of the group through a vote of the attending members. Or someone at such a meeting may make a motion that the chair appoint a conference committee or various other committees. (See also the discussions about committees in the second part of the book, "Meeting Conduct: The New Robert's Rules of Order.")

In an office situation, a manager or department head might make all decisions about appointments or assignments. Or a board of directors might appoint a conference chair who in turn would appoint an executive committee that in turn would appoint various other committees or subcommittees (finance, program, and so on).

Regardless of how your organization operates and whatever authority you have to proceed alone, one person or a committee, or various people or various committees, will have to be responsible for some or all of these functions:

- Planning
- Finance
- Program development
- Speakers
- Meeting notices and agendas
- Publicity and promotion

- Registration
- Site and facilities
- Equipment and presentation aids
- Exhibits and demonstrations
- Meals and entertainment
- Minutes and proceedings

These items are described in the chapters that follow. For information about the formation of a new organization and first and second meetings, refer to Section 48 in the second part of the book on meeting conduct.

4. FINANCES

Financial Requirements

Planners need to know who's in charge of the money. If your meeting is large enough to involve expenses, someone has to be responsible for the fiscal aspect of the arrangements.

Although a small meeting in your office may not involve more than a cup of coffee or a soft drink—perhaps purchased out of the office petty-cash fund—a larger meeting could involve room and equipment rental, catering-service charges, transportation costs, and other expenses. When a meeting involves such things, it clearly points to the need for a budget and one or more persons in charge of financial record keeping and disbursements.

Financial control of a meeting can be handled in various ways depending on certain factors: the type and size of the meeting, the number of expense categories involved, the prior existence of a financial officer in your organization who always handles meeting finance, and any rules or regulations of your organization that specify a required procedure.

The Finance Committee. Assume that you have been appointed finance chair in a national organization that's planning to hold a three-day meeting in Cleveland. What should you do? (See also Section 52 in the second part of the book on meeting conduct.)

Ask for instructions on handling finances from the Planning Committee or from the specific person(s) to whom you'll be reporting, such as the meeting chair or coordinator. Be certain to find out whether the meeting is expected to be a money maker or a break-even event or whether it's expected to operate at a loss to the organization. Not all meetings are intended to make money; some serve an indirect purpose, such as company enhancement, or fill a nonprofit, educational need.

Review the bylaws or other rules and regulations of your organization to see if any requirements apply to financial matters in a meeting. For example, perhaps the secretary of the organization must always approve all expenditures and the treasurer always sign all checks. As soon as you know what you may and may not do and who does what in regard to approving final expenditures and paying the incoming bills, you're ready to go to work.

First Committee Meeting. If you have been instructed to form your own committee and if the proposed meeting is large enough to warrant other members (in addition to your own office assistants), you will begin here. Select one to three other persons to form the committee and call a first meeting. Explain the ground rules to them—the do's and don'ts of your organization—and cover the following points (you may do more or less than this to the extent that your own meeting differs from this example):

- Discuss the preliminary meeting plans and schedule—proposed meeting dates and sessions, probable number of speakers, desired number of attendees, and so on.

- Give the members a list of the other committees and names, addresses, and telephone numbers of the chairs.

- Describe the duties and procedures of finance committees that worked on previous meetings.

- Give members a copy of the budget used for a previous, similar meeting as an example.

- List the tasks and steps concerning finance that you anticipate for the upcoming meeting.

- Assign specific tasks, with priorities, to the other committee members. For example, each person may be responsible for collecting information pertaining to certain expense items (hotels, meals, printing, promotion, and so on) in the budget.

• Discuss any other tasks, procedures, or pertinent matters. Include on-site rules and procedures (does the organization allow, or will you allow, registrants to cash checks or use credit cards?) as well as pre-meeting committee procedures.

• Set a date for the next committee meeting, at which time members should report their activity to date and further steps should be defined.

Some committee members will have people from their own office staffs to help in collecting, organizing, and recording data. But each member will be responsible for his or her own assignments, and you as the finance chair will be responsible for the overall work of your committee.

Coordination with Other Committees. As soon as possible, schedule a time to meet individually or all together with other committee chairs to exchange information and to be certain that everyone is working in unison. If individuals are in separate locations, set up a time to hold a long-distance telephone or computer conference (see Chapter 2). If the Planning Committee has appointed a meeting coordinator, this person will help to maintain smooth, consistent operations and regular contacts with other committees.

Avoid delays, since the other committees have to know their fiscal limits in order to pursue their assigned arrangements. Estimated costs, for example, will affect decisions about what to charge as a registration fee.

The Meeting Budget

You need to ask for an individual budget from each committee to use in preparing your own overall meeting budget. Each committee, therefore, must work out a budget pertaining to its assigned area. In the case of hotel arrangements, for example, you don't have to go to the hotel representative yourself to find out the various estimated hotel costs for the meeting. The Facilities Committee is responsible for making such contacts and collecting such data for you. However, you must incorporate the Facilities Committee's budget into your own overall meeting budget.

Once you have all the committee budgets—and have worked with the committees in solving any related problems—you're ready to prepare the general meeting budget. This overall budget should then be presented to the Planning Committee for approval.

Depending on the size of the proposed meeting, your budget may include numerous items. For a large conference, it will include room rental, meals and other refreshments, gratuities, entertainment, airport transportation, equipment rental, telephone, postage, stationery, addressing and mailing, printing, photocopying, speaker fees, parking, and anything else needed before, during, and after the meeting.

An organization arranging a large conference will have accounting and spreadsheet computer programs that can be used in handling the financial matters of the conference. Therefore, if you set up your expense categories with a computer, you can change your figures at a moment's notice and quickly print a revised budget at any time.

Spreadsheet Format. If your organization doesn't have a standard computer format that you must follow for the budget, devise your own arrangement of data in a columnar format. List the expenses (rooms, meals, and so on) in the left-hand column and across the page have a row of expense columns. Head the first expense column "Proposed Expenditures," and head the next few columns "Revised Expenditures." Fill in your revised figures in the blank columns each time you have to change the budget.

Head the next three to six columns "Expenditures to Date." Use these columns to record how much has been spent as of certain dates. Head the final column "Total [*or* Actual] Expenditures." There, you'll record the sum of all bills paid for each category listed in the first column (meals, equipment rental, and so on). After all figures are finally available, add up the amounts in each column and note the totals at the bottom.

Expenses	Proposed Expend.	Rev. Expend.	Expend. To Date	Total Expend.
(1)	(1)	(1) (2) etc.	(1) (2) (3) etc.	(1)

Budget Revisions. Be prepared to make revisions. Portions of the budget may not satisfy the Planning Committee. Perhaps the proposed printing expenditure looks too high to the committee, or perhaps the meals figure looks too low. In such cases, you'll have to go back to the committees in charge of printing and meals and work out revised figures. Continue with this procedure until, finally, your overall budget is approved.

As soon as the budget is approved, notify the other committees concerning their own areas of concern. You may, however, have to submit several revised budgets as certain committees advise you from time to time that their original estimates are proving to be inaccurate. To avoid too much of this, the Planning Committee should insist that committees secure signed contracts from vendors with prices clearly defined and not subject to change.

Let the other committee chairs know how much they may spend on their own, without authorization from the Planning Committee or from your Finance Committee, and which expenses must first be approved. Establish guidelines for them in regard to ordering supplies (ask for a written request with related cost estimates), prepaying vendors (don't do it unless it was agreed to in a signed contract), submission of receipts to you (all receipts from the various committees should promptly go to you or other designated person), and so on.

Financial Reports

Throughout the period of meeting preparation, you will be reporting regularly to the Planning Committee. Indicate the work status of your committee and present an updated statement of income (from registrations, for example) and expenses.

If you set up the income and expense categories on a computer, you can regularly insert revised figures and print an updated statement at any time. However, if your organization doesn't have a computer program for preparing such reports, follow the example of statements submitted in previous meetings of your organization. Or simply prepare a basic list of income received by category (registration fees, sales of publications, and so on) and then expenses by category (supplies, speaker fees, and so on), with net profit or loss to date (total income to date minus total expenses to date).

Receivables and Payables

Establish a procedure for recording and depositing receipts and for approving bills for payment. Your organization may require that you immediately turn over all receipts to an accounting department or to the person designated as bookkeeper or treasurer. But you still need to keep your own records of registrations paid and to be billed as well as a current list of bills paid and due.

The exact recording procedure used should be established in conjunction with the accounting department's requirements, the format of your computer program, and your own need for fiscal monitoring and control. No matter who actually does the bookkeeping, income and expenses must be recorded according to the method required in your organization.

Be certain that everyone (on your committee and on other committees) closely reads what outside contracts require in regard to when payment is due. That is, when does a deposit or a final check have to be drawn, and is the contract consistent with your organization's own rules and procedures?

If the committees don't take care in contracting, bills may be due and payable before enough receipts have come in to cover them. Or you may have the reverse problem: It takes so long for bills to come in or for committees to submit them to you that you can't properly monitor and control the handling and reporting of income and expenses in a timely manner. You may even have to ask for bills in order to prepare required financial reports on schedule.

After the meeting, you will need to take care of the final unpaid bills, see that on-site or late registration fees and other receipts are deposited, and—finally—close the files and records for this meeting. Again, coordinate this aspect closely with your accounting department or with the designated bookkeeper or treasurer.

As soon as you've taken care of the last details, undertake a postmeeting evaluation of financial matters and committee activities for use in handling future meetings, and submit a final income and expense report to the Planning Committee.

5. PROGRAM DEVELOPMENT

Program Planning

Organizations plan programs to present to members and invited guests as well as to the general public. Your local culture club may hold an arts-and-crafts show with competitive entries, judges, noncompetitive displays, guest speakers, and other features. A school may prepare a recital for parents, teachers, and the community at large. A company may provide an orientation program for new employees or a product demonstration for customers and prospects. A national association may hold an annual conference with numerous speakers and sessions.

For any such event, some person or committee will have to develop a program. The more complex the meeting, the more that the person or committee will have to do.

The Program Committee. Consider again the example described in the previous chapter of a national organization holding a three-day meeting in Cleveland. This time, assume that you're in charge of program development. What do you do first?

Follow the example of the Finance Committee described in the previous chapter. Review any instructions you receive from the Planning Committee, study the by-laws and any other rules and regulations of your organization, and examine the correspondence and reports of previous program committees and the printed programs they developed.

For a meeting of this complexity, a committee of several people will be needed. The work is more than one person alone can handle, especially if that person also has a full-time job elsewhere.

At your first meeting, follow the example of the Finance Committee's first meeting. Discuss preliminary plans and scheduling, give your committee members an address list of the other committee chairs, tell them about the duties and procedures of previous program committees, show them copies of previous programs, list the tasks you anticipate for your committee, make committee task assignments (perhaps each person will be working on a certain portion of the program), and set a date for the next committee meeting.

If the proposed three-day meeting in Cleveland has a coordinator (it probably does), meet with that person to establish working procedures and then meet regularly thereafter. If there's no coordinator, take the initiative yourself and open communication channels to the various committees (site and facilities, meals, equipment, registration, and so on). You'll be developing a program consistent with their activities.

The Program

Although many meetings have different needs and hence require different planning procedures, you'll no doubt be preparing an organized program of events and all related aspects, from registration details to hotel accommodations. This program presumably will be printed and mailed to interested persons who may want to attend the meeting in Cleveland.

Another person or committee may be in charge of printing and mailing, or each committee may handle its own printing and mailing requirements. Regardless of the practice in your organization, your task is to develop a three-day program to be presented in as-yet-undetermined facilities in Cleveland.

By now, the Planning Committee has probably suggested a theme and stated its objectives. The Finance Committee either has or will request a proposed Program Committee budget from you. When the overall meeting budget is approved by the Planning Committee, the Finance Committee will let you know exactly what expenses you may incur (speakers' fees; telephone, fax, and postage costs; and so on), which ones require authorization, and how to handle ongoing budget revisions.

In the meantime, you can be clarifying certain program details within your own committee. If you haven't been given a specific title for the conference, what titles can your committee suggest to the Planning Committee? (The Publicity and Promotion Committee will be interested in such details also.) How would you characterize the expected audience and how will you reach it? This may be the responsibility of the Publicity and Promotion Committee, but you'll nevertheless need to work closely with anyone who has to get the news of your program out to the selected audience.

The Meeting Objective. You'll be directly concerned with the objective of the meeting. Is it to provide an educational program for your organization's membership and other interested parties? To provide a forum for interested persons to exchange new developments and techniques in your field? To solve problems that affect everyone in the industry or profession? Something else?

Meetings often have more than one objective, as indicated in Chapter 3, but regardless of the number, the purpose of the meeting is your guide to the program— the topics for discussion that you'll set up, the speakers you'll need, and so on. It also is a key to the audience that will be contacted while soliciting attendance.

Times and Dates. Times and dates are two things of major importance to the Program Committee. You need to deal in specifics, not generalities. Precisely, when does on-site registration begin and end? Chaos will erupt if your schedule isn't stated accurately. Precisely, when does this or that session start and end in this or that specific room and on which day? Precisely, when is there a refreshment break? Precisely, when is the Tuesday luncheon speaker to be introduced and brought to the podium?

Your program for each day should begin with breakfast or the first scheduled event or action. Include the exact time that certain doors will open or when an information, publications sales, or registration booth will open for business. Entertainment or special events for spouses and attendees should also be included (select events such as tours and dinner-dances that appeal to both men and women), as well as day-care arrangements.

Activity Schedule. If your organization has a planning and scheduling computer program, you'll already have a format for scheduling the activities. Otherwise, look for a suitable printed form in a conference-planning book, or devise your own format and save it in your computer.

Some program chairs list times for activities in ten- or fifteen-minute increments in the left-hand column of an activity schedule. Across the top of the page, for example, you may have five columns—three for the three days of the proposed meeting and first and last columns for the day before the meeting and the day after. Some things, such as transportation to and from the airport, will be listed on the day before or after. By using a computer, you can easily revise the titles of topics and their order and print out an updated schedule at a moment's notice.

Sessions and Topics. You'll need a lot of brainstorming sessions with your own committee—and others—to select the best mix of topics for the workshops and other sessions, including prospective speakers. The Planning Committee may give you only a general theme and sample topics or certain essential topics that it definitely wants you to include. It will then be up to you and your committee to spell out a well-rounded mix and arrange the topics over the three days to give people clear and convenient choices for the sessions they want to attend.

Some sessions may be parallel—two or more running at the same time in different rooms. This type of meeting presents a problem. Although traffic control may not be your responsibility, you need to consider it in scheduling sessions to avoid bottlenecks and confusion.

"To Be Announced." It's not likely that you will be able to confirm every topic and have speakers committed

to handle all topics by the time you need to print and mail an advance program and registration packet. Although all program committees dislike having to state "To Be Announced" in a topic or speaker slot on a program, it may be unavoidable in some cases.

If your audience is widely scattered geographically and you're mailing packets at a less-expensive but slower bulk rate, the program mailing may be scheduled two to three months before the meeting. This is necessary to reach people early enough for them to be able to register and make travel and other arrangements.

Speakers may not be immediately available to give you an answer in time. However, if they're prominent persons, you may elect to wait for their replies rather than select someone of lesser stature who might be able to give you a faster yes or no.

For details about arrangements for speakers, see the discussion in the following pages of this chapter; for information on the printing and mailing of program packages, see the material on publicity and promotion in the next chapter.

Progress Reports

Throughout your work in developing a program, you should report your progress regularly to the Planning Committee. Also, work closely with the meeting coordinator (if any) or the chairs of the various committees (facilities, meals, and so on) who will be providing details to you to go in the program.

The Planning Committee will probably expect you to submit a list of proposed topics and events and a tentative time-date schedule as well as a proposed list of speakers and assigned topics. This list of topics must be approved before you have a program printed. The speaker list also should be approved before you issue invitations to speakers. In all of these matters, however, follow the required procedure in your organization.

The Speakers

Meeting arrangers rely on guest speakers for many types of meeting programs. A local chamber of commerce may want someone to speak about community development at a luncheon meeting. An investment firm may want several in-house employees or outside speakers to address the attendees at a seminar for investors. A retail trade association may hold a major conference or convention that has numerous sessions with guest speakers.

The larger and more complex the meeting, the more that you have to do to make speaker arrangements. But regardless of meeting complexity, you want to be certain that you pick the right people and provide what they need to make their speeches and presentations a success.

Data Forms. The person in charge of program development or the Program Committee for an upcoming meeting often handles the arrangements for speakers. The Planning Committee may or may not give you instructions for this. Either way, you'll find that the use of data forms will simplify your task.

If your computer has a conference-planning program, examine its forms pertaining to committee use and those for the use of speakers. Also, look at the files on previous meetings to see whether your organization has any such special forms that you should use or adapt to your needs. However, if you don't have appropriate forms on your computer and can't find any in the files, look for samples in a conference planning guide or devise some on your own.

Consider what information you'll need to know. For example, for each topic on your program, you'll need to know what special requirements are involved, what background or education a speaker must have to address a particular topic, what enhancements the topic requires (filmstrips, copy boards, audience participation, and so on), and the names of likely candidates for speaking on a particular topic.

The Committee Data Form. If you're devising your own forms, use your computer to set up a spreadsheet type of format for recording data for committee needs. Prepare at least one such form on which you can record all pertinent information about the topics and the associated speakers and requirements.

In the left-hand column, for example, list each topic (with date and times). Across the top, head the various columns with the pertinent items, such as supplies needed (for speakers or for audiences), equipment needed (such as computers or audiovisuals), special speaker qualifications (education, job experience, and so on), prospective candidates, sources of candidates (direct company contacts, speaker bureaus, directories, and so on), and any other data you'll need to know.

Topic	Date, Time	**Requirements** Supplies Equipment [Etc.]	**Speakers** Prospects Sources

Have each of your committee members fill in this data sheet. You can then combine all of their suggested equipment needs, suggestions for speakers, and other requirements on one master chart.

In addition, don't hesitate to ask others working on the meeting arrangements for suggestions or to use any other source you can think of to solicit speaker recommendations. Most meeting planners prefer to have personal recommendations, but if none are forthcoming, you may want to peruse the trade press for names or consult appropriate directories such an those of the National Speakers' Association or Meeting Planners International. Also check your Yellow Pages for nearby speakers' bureaus.

The Speaker-Evaluation Form. If your meeting is large and complex, you'll probably need several other forms, including a speaker-evaluation form. This form provides you and others a place to answer questions about suggested speakers and their suitability for the program. For example:

- What qualifications or credentials does the person have to speak on the proposed topic?

- Was the individual recommended by someone?

- Is the person an effective speaker?

- What speaking fee will the person expect?

- Is the person likely to be available?

- Will the person, by reputation, enhance the program?

As you study the evaluation forms completed by members of your committee and others, consider whether the complete roster of speakers provides the mix you want in terms of gender, age, experience, religion, race, education, and geographic representation.

Not many organizations today would want to hold a meeting at which the speakers were all white Protestant males from New York City. As you think about the mix you're developing, decide whether you want a variety that will reflect the composition of your audience.

When you have matched one or more names of prospective candidates to the program topics, rank them in order of preference. Put a number *1* by your first choice, a *2* by your second choice, and so on.

Although you may not have talked to any of the prospective speakers at this point, experts recommend that you never invite someone to speak without confirming that the person meets your requirements. Résumés, personal videos, and other material prepared by the prospective speaker will show only the person's best side. You need to know more than that. Usually this means that you must meet with or at least telephone the candidate and people who know the person.

When you're satisfied with your choices, submit your list to the Planning Committee for approval. Once you have authorization to proceed, you are ready to prepare the speaker invitations.

The Speaker Data Form. You'll need either a single data sheet for the speakers to fill out or separate sheets—one for biographical information and one for the speaker's equipment and supplies requests. A data sheet should include the usual lines for the speaker's name, address, telephone/fax/E-mail numbers, company affiliation, and so on. It also should have a place where speakers can check off (or fill in) their equipment, lighting, and other needs. (See the discussion of an equipment checklist in Chapter 7.)

Don't rely on speakers to tell you everything without a form to guide them. Providing a standard, easy-to-complete form is mandatory. To avoid the confusion of missing or incomplete information, be certain that all speakers fill out the necessary form or forms completely, and be certain that they all use the same form rather than their own forms. This is important so that you'll have consistent information.

Speaker Invitations. If your organization has on file copies of previous correspondence with speakers, you can use them as a guide. Otherwise, first prepare a basic letter of invitation (to speak at the meeting) that will be suitable for most of your initial speaker contacts.

You may want to prepare an information sheet about the meeting and its sponsor to send to the speakers. If you have a separate brochure describing your organization, it also can be enclosed along with the speaker invitation and the information sheet. Include the following details on the information sheet:

- The meeting theme and title
- The meeting dates
- The meeting location
- A capsule of the expected audience and number attending
- Your organization's policy concerning fees or honorariums
- The policy concerning expense reimbursement and transportation fees for speakers
- Other general information a speaker should know

Close with the name, address, and telephone number of someone the speaker may contact for further details.

If you put all of this routine information on an enclosed information sheet, you can confine your letters to the speakers to the basic invitation or details that apply to a particular speaker: the person's topic and any desired slant or emphasis, the date and exact time of that person's presentation, and so on. If you don't have such a sheet to enclose, your letter will have to be much longer and more detailed.

If you have enclosures with the letter of invitation, such as data sheets to be completed or a contract to be signed, remember to ask the speaker to return each item by a certain date and to send any information or material you need.

For example, you may need a current photograph and biographical summary, the precise title of the speaker's address, and so on in time to be included in the printed program. Otherwise, you'll have to omit the data in the program or guess at it. You will also need a list of supplies and equipment the speaker will need in time to make rental and setup arrangements, and you may need a copy of the speaker's address in time to include it in a printed copy of all conference addresses.

If a written copy of the speaker's paper is needed for inclusion in a published book of conference proceedings, the speaker will need to know your requirements. They will include details such as the allowable length, number and type of photographs, and writing style (subheads, footnotes, and so on), as well as the deadline for submission. (See the discussion of proceedings in Chapter 8.)

A speaker data form, described earlier, that all speakers complete will make it easier for everyone. If they don't have such a form to complete, you can be certain that some of them will forget to tell you something or will miss a deadline.

Other Speaker Contacts. The correspondence from an organization to a speaker will be signed by either the Program Committee chair or the conference chair (a contract is usually signed by the conference chair). The number of letters, you write to the speakers depends on the type of meeting. In addition to the initial invitation letter described previously, the following letters are common in many types and sizes of meetings.

- A *confirmation letter* acknowledging the speaker's acceptance (or refusal, if that's the case) and restating the facts about the speaker's presentation (topic, objectives, date, time, and so on). Enclose a contract (if used) and forms for the speaker to complete, such as a speaker's data form (described previously) or separate biographical data form and supplies and equipment checklist (see the discussion of equipment and presentation aids in Chapter 7). Have space on the form or forms for the speaker to indicate any desired room setup (see the discussion of site and facilities arrangements in Chapter 7).

- A *welcome letter* to serve as a cover letter with the packet of information given to speakers arriving at the meeting. This packet should include necessary materials, such as a printed program, an expense form, a name tag, a map of the meeting facilities, and any other material or information a speaker will need at the site.

- A *thank-you letter,* sent after the meeting, complimenting the speaker on his or her outstanding contribution.

The Speaker Contract. Organizations that hold large, complex conferences usually have formal contracts that spell out the arrangement between a speaker and the organization in charge of a conference. This type of contract, if used, should be sent to a speaker in duplicate and should be signed by both the speaker and the conference chair. One of the signed copies will be kept by or be returned to the speaker.

Usually, such an agreement states the meeting theme or title, the date, and the location. It should also list details concerning the speaker's presentation—title, time, and date—as well as any financial, transportation, billing, or other arrangements for the speaker. Include any applicable terms in case of cancellation by the speaker.

Although formal contracts are common for large conferences, they are used less often for smaller meetings. Many organizations that hold small meetings consider a routine exchange of correspondence to be a sufficient understanding of the terms of the arrangement and each party's commitment. Nevertheless, a specific letter of agreement is always added insurance that there will be no misunderstanding later.

Speaker Cancellations. Regardless of how many forms you believe you need for your meeting or what type of formal or informal arrangements you need with the speakers, one caution applies in all cases. Everyone who makes arrangements for even one speaker shares the concern that there will be a late cancellation. Knowing that this is a possibility, you can save yourself a lot of trouble if you arrange for standby speakers.

Sometimes members of the committees arranging a conference or members of their organizations prepare addresses—just in case. Or outside speakers may be selected and invited to serve as alternates or standbys. These persons may be prepared to speak on the scheduled topic, or they may have another topic to address. In any case, the standbys should receive all of the same literature that a scheduled speaker receives. This will prevent the need for extensive last-minute briefing.

Any late program changes must be announced to the attendees as soon as possible, perhaps at a breakfast gathering. If an information booth or a bulletin board is set up in the lobby, immediately post any such changes and report them to the Planning Committee. Also, be prepared to make the necessary supplies and equipment changes or any other changes necessitated by the unexpected cancellation.

After all changes are made and the program has been concluded, send participating speakers a thank you letter, complete your committee duties, prepare a post-meeting evaluation report for use in future meetings, and send a final report to the Planning Committee. Refer to the next chapter for a description of the program printing and mailing arrangements.

6. ATTENDEE CONTACTS

Notices and Agendas

First Attendee Contacts. For an upcoming meeting, usually the first things that prospective attendees receive are a notice of the meeting and an agenda—a list of topics to be presented or discussed. When a meeting is large and complex, such as a conference with multiple sessions and numerous guest speakers, the organizers must prepare a detailed notice and agenda.

Typically, the organizers of a complex conference prepare a formal program (see Chapter 5) and mail it in advance to prospective registrants, along with registration details. This advance program-registration package serves as both a notice of the upcoming meeting and the agenda for the overall conference. (See also the discussion of publicity and promotion in this chapter.)

During the program, however, the board of directors of the organization and various committees may hold small meetings of their own to transact pertinent business. Notices of such meetings and the associated agendas are handled apart from the general meeting announcement and program.

The Meeting Notice. A meeting notice is required for meetings of all sizes. You may simply want to meet with one or two people in your home or office. Or you may need to hold a larger organized meeting to discuss something or to transact business that requires the concurrence or vote of other members of your group. To arrange for a meeting of any size, you need to announce the date, time, and place.

If you just want to talk to someone in your office,

the notice will likely consist of a telephone call, a brief conventional letter or memo, or a fax or E-mail message. You will probably ask the recipient if it will be convenient to meet in your office at a certain time on a certain day to discuss a particular matter. The agenda for such a meeting may consist only of some personal penciled notes to help remind you of points you want to make or questions you want to ask.

Combination Notice-Proxy. Assume that you have in mind something that is larger than a simple office meeting with another person. Perhaps it's time to hold a meeting of the board of directors of your local business association. If the bylaws of your organization specify that the secretary is to call, or announce, such meetings, and you are the secretary, you will prepare some type of formal notice. Perhaps your organization has always sent such notices in the form of business letters.

If the meeting is even larger, however, perhaps including the entire membership, you may have announcements printed and send them with or without a proxy enclosed. (A *proxy* is an authorization given to someone else allowing the other person to vote for you in your absence.) A combination notice-proxy is another option. In this case, the notice is stated first, and a proxy follows immediately after it on the same card or sheet.

NOTICE

Members of the Business Association are hereby notified that the next meeting of the association will be held in Princeton, New Jersey, at the Frontier Inn, on January 19, 19XX, at 7:30 p.m. If you will be unable to attend, please sign this stamped, self-addressed proxy card and return it promptly.

PROXY

I hereby constitute David Jordan, Marilee Addington, and Louis Pradella, who are officers or directors of the association, or a majority of such of them as actually are present, to act for me in my stead and as my proxy at the January

meeting of the Business Association, to be held in Princeton, New Jersey, at the Frontier Inn, on January 19, 19XX, at 7:30 p.m., and at any adjournment or adjournments thereof, with full power and authority to act for me in my behalf, with all powers that I, the undersigned, would possess if I were personally present.

Effective Date_____
Signed_____
City_____State_____Zip Code_____

PLEASE BE CERTAIN TO COMPLETE THE ABOVE FORM IN FULL BEFORE MAILING. NO POSTAGE IS REQUIRED. THANK YOU.

Proxies are important when it's likely that not enough members will be present at the meeting to constitute the quorum required to transact business. The notice and proxy form do not have to be combined, however. Follow the preferred practice in your organization or any requirements stated in the bylaws.

Reply Cards. Use announcements of previous meetings as your guide in preparing the current announcement. For example, perhaps your organization has always enclosed a check-off attendance reply card. With such a card, the member will fill in his or her name and address and check the appropriate place for designating intentions.

I will ( ) will not ( ) attend the January 19, 19XX, meeting of the Business Association.

Name_____Date_____
Address_____
_____

PLEASE COMPLETE AND RETURN BY DECEMBER 31, 19XX.

This type of reply card can be especially useful if you're holding a luncheon or dinner meeting and you need to know in advance how many meals to order. Regardless of the type of meeting, however, remember to give on the card or in the accompanying notice a deadline for returning the card.

The Meeting Agenda. Meetings of all sizes have a formal agenda (also called "order of business") or informal list of topics to be discussed, depending on the formality and size of the meeting. Like the meeting notice, the agenda should be prepared according to the format required or preferred by your organization. Use examples from previous meetings as a guide.

Sometimes the meeting chair or secretary solicits items for the agenda before preparing it. A board of directors, for instance, that meets infrequently will want to be certain that it doesn't forget anything and that everyone has an opportunity to add matters of importance to the agenda.

If you hold the position of secretary or presiding officer on the board and are responsible for preparing the agenda, write to other members of the board. State that you're preparing the agenda and that if anyone has any topic to be included, he or she should send it to you by a certain date.

For events such as board meetings, your organization may distribute advance copies of the agenda so that everyone can study the topics and be prepared to act on the items. It can save time during a meeting if people are given an opportunity to do their homework before the meeting begins.

Start preparing the agenda early, in sufficient time for an exchange of correspondence with others before the meeting. Some people start preparing an agenda for the next meeting the day after the previous meeting has ended. Store your rough drafts on the computer so that you can easily make numerous additions and deletions and quickly print an up-to-date copy at any time.

Selection of Topics. Which items you should put on an agenda will depend on the type of meeting and its objectives. If it's time to elect new officers, that item will be prominent on the agenda; otherwise, it will be omitted.

Study the organization's bylaws carefully to determine any requirements that will affect the topics listed and the format, general preparation procedure, and distribution. If any members to whom you are sending copies of the agenda are coming from out of town, you may additionally want to enclose a map, with directions marked to the meeting site, as well as recommendations for transportation or overnight accommodations.

The agenda for a semiformal or formal meeting may have some or all of the following topics (or additional topics). State the organization's name and the date, time, and place of the meeting in a heading preceding the list of topics. In a formal agenda, you may also want to assign times to the various topics and state the allotted time in front of each item on the agenda.

AGENDA

Business Association
January 19, 19XX, 7:30 p.m.
Frontier Inn
Princeton, NJ 08540

Call to order
Reading, correction, and approval of previous
  minutes
Reading of correspondence
Officers' reports
Executive committee report
Standing committees' reports
Special committees' reports
Unfinished [old] business
New business
Appointment of committees
Announcements
Adjournment

Both the preliminary agenda and the final agenda may contain more detailed listings. Under "officers' reports," for example, you may list each officer—treasurer, first vice-president, and so on—who is reporting. Under "unfinished business," you may want to list the specific items being carried over from a previous meeting. Under "new business," you will likely list the specific new topics to be brought up.

Meeting File. The presiding officer should have a file with even more detailed information concerning each agenda item. All members, in fact, may want to prepare notes on a meeting folder with reports and any other data they may need to refer to in order to vote on matters and comment intelligently. (See also "Officers and Committees" and "Introduction of Business" in the second part of the book on meeting conduct.)

Publicity and Promotion

To reach prospective attendees, some meetings require extensive promotion and need as much publicity as possible to ensure success. In other cases, publicity and promotion would be inappropriate. One wouldn't hold a press conference, for example, or do a mass mailing to announce the regular Monday morning meeting of your office staff or the quarterly meeting of the First Lutheran Church Board of Directors.

Any meeting that relies on the participation of the general public or large numbers of interested persons, however, has to be announced to the prospective audience in some way (see the preceding discussion of meeting notices). It needs more than a simple telephone call or letter to a few people; it needs strategic publicity and promotion to a wider audience to ensure adequate attendance.

The Publicity and Promotion Committee. Organizations that hold large meetings, such as a trade show or conference, usually have a separate promotion or publicity and promotion committee. In some cases, the Program Committee (see Chapter 5) handles publicity and promotion. In other cases, when the meeting is not complex, one person alone may be appointed to handle this part of the meeting arrangements.

Assume, as you did in Chapters 4 and 5, that you're

a member of a national organization that is arranging a large, three-day meeting in Cleveland. The Planning Committee has just appointed you to serve as the chair of the Publicity and Promotion Committee. Where do you start? Your first step will be to select one to three persons to serve on your committee and to call a meeting of the committee as soon as possible.

Brief yourself, however, before you hold the first meeting of your committee and attempt to brief the members. Review instructions you received from the Planning Committee, read the bylaws and any other rules of your organization that might affect your committee, and meet with other key organizers, such as the meeting chair, the meeting coordinator, and the finance chair.

The finance chair will no doubt ask you to submit a proposed budget for your committee. Upon approval of this budget, the finance chair will let you know how much you may spend, for which items you'll need prior authorization, and so on. Review the preliminary steps for a committee described in Chapter 4.

During your first committee meeting, give the members an address list of the other committee chairs and tell them about the meeting's theme, objectives, and desired audience. Explain what previous promotion committees did and what you want to do for the Cleveland meeting. Provide the members with a schedule and suggested deadlines. Finally, assign tasks to individual members, but give them a chance to make their own suggestions as well.

Printing and Mailing. One committee member may be in charge of securing quotes and schedules from printers or company desktop (computer) publishing departments. This should cover any literature to be printed, such as an early announcement, the main pre-meeting program-registration packet mailed to prospective attendees, and a final program booklet distributed to registrants at the conference.

Someone else may look into sources of mailing lists. For example, does your organization maintain its own list of prospects, or will you have to buy or rent outside lists from mailing-list vendors? Perhaps you retained lists used in previous conferences and have them stored in a company database.

The person investigating mailing lists may also look into in-house or outside services for addressing and mailing the promotional packets. This person may additionally secure quotes and the required timetable for mailings, as well as determine postal costs and requirements. Does your organization have or need to apply for a special bulk-mailing permit?

Outside Services. Perhaps you'll assign yourself the task of exploring various outside services or options. For example, you may decide to retain a public relations company or an advertising firm to prepare promotional packages and to arrange for the mailings; for the press releases, radio announcements, television spots, and Internet announcements; and for any premeeting or onsite press conferences.

You may also want to explore the possibility of receiving promotional assistance from an airline. Some airlines, for example, may be willing to do a promotional mailing for your conference free of charge or at a reduced cost if you will also declare it to be the "official" airline for that meeting.

Cost-Saving Measures. Since costs are always a concern, the committee members should get several quotes for items such as printing and mailing and submit them to you. After reviewing these estimates, you may decide that budget limitations make it necessary to rule out the use of certain outside services, such as a public relations or advertising firm.

If you need to introduce cost-saving measures, you may decide to write your own press releases, prepare any other promotional material that you need, and handle printing or desktop publishing arrangements on your own. However, you and the other committee members will probably have a personal office staff to help you do routine tasks, such as proofreading printed material and mailing press releases.

Depending on your budget limitations, you and your committee members may have to handle nearly everything. You may have to develop the strategies; prepare a schedule for program printing and mailings, press release mailings, and other types of publicity and promotion; supervise the entire operation; and coordinate your committee's work with other key players, such as the program chair, the finance chair, and the person in charge of advance and on-site registration. (If a meeting coordinator is available, your job may be much easier.)

Data Collection. Much of the information you collect will come from other committees. The Program Committee, for example, should give you a draft of the three-day program. The Registration Committee (or person on the Program Committee in charge of registration) should provide copy for the registration instructions and the card or form that registrants are supposed to fill out and return with their registration fees.

These committees and others should also give you information about other matters. This information will include details on hotel accommodations, transportation to and from the airports, a site map, entertainment for participants and spouses, day-care facilities at the conference site, accommodations for the handicapped, publications and other items to be sold at the meeting, and special features or unusual events, such as a tour.

If the Program Committee hasn't organized this mix of information, it will be up to you to put it in proper order for the proposed brochure or other conference mailer, to edit it to size so that the packet to be mailed won't be too large or heavy for your mailing budget, and to work with an outside printer or in-house desktop operator on all of this. If you retain a public relations or advertising firm to handle the printing and mailing, however, someone else will take care of these details.

A committee member who works for a company with an in-house desktop publishing department may be able to arrange for preparation of the mailer at no cost to you. But whether you use in-house desktop publishing or an outside printer, be certain to ask how you should submit the material to be produced. Perhaps the operator will need a computer disk copy of your material as well as a double-spaced manuscript.

Scheduling. Regardless of who prepares the promotional material, your schedule must take into account the time required for packages to reach prospects and the time they need to get company authorization to attend the event and send in their registration fees. Ask your local post office about the time required for mailing at an economical bulk rate.

Work closely in regard to schedules with the Program Committee and the Registration Committee. Since you can't get anything printed and mailed until they give you the information you need, it's important that everyone understands your deadlines. Once you have collected all the information you need and have everything put together, submit a rough design of your proposed packet to the Planning Committee for approval.

Press Releases. If you plan to use paid advertising in magazines or trade journals and newspapers, as well as on the radio or over television, you will probably retain an advertising agency to create and place the ads for you (unless a committee member volunteers the services of his or her employer's ad department). In any case, you may decide to write your own press releases to announce the upcoming meeting.

Stick to the essential facts about the meeting—time, date, and place; type of meeting, such as a technical conference; important features, including prominent speakers; and other *essential* data. Follow the examples of press release used for previous meetings.

Does your organization have a press release letterhead? If not, use the organization's regular business stationery. Observe the key elements of an effective release (one that will be accepted and printed). If your organization doesn't already have a press mailing list, consult a directory of magazines, newspapers, radio and television stations, and so on in a local library reference room (ask the reference librarian for help in locating what you need).

Press Release Preparation. Double-space all pages on the release and type "—more—" at the end of each page that is to be continued on another page. Keep the release as succinct as possible and put the paragraphs in order of importance. This is important, because editors cut from the bottom up. For example, if you have ten paragraphs, an editor may delete the last eight and keep the first two.

At the top right on the first page, just below the printed letterhead, identify someone the press can contact in your organization for more information:

For further information:
John Jones, 602-555-1004

Add an address for John Jones if his address is different from the letterhead address.

A couple inches down, center the date you are releasing the information (often, "immediately"):

FOR IMMEDIATE RELEASE

The press prefers to write its own headlines, so you can omit that information, if desired. In that case, begin with a dateline placed at the beginning of the first paragraph (include where the release originates from and the date):

DETROIT, MICH., March 11, 19XX: The twenty-sixth annual meeting and technical conference of the . . .

Use straightforward language—no sensational adjectives, such as *tremendous* or *amazing*. If appropriate, enclose a photograph. Perhaps a revolutionary new product will be unveiled at the meeting. Send an eight-by-ten-inch black-and-white glossy photograph. At the end of the release, write "—30—" or "END."

If the release runs onto a second or third page, use either printed second-page stationery that matches the letterhead page or use a plain sheet of paper. In either case, place the page number at the top right and a word or two summarizing the subject of the release at the top left.

Although you may be mailing to numerous journals and newspapers, all with different deadlines for the next issue, keep in mind that a release must reach a publication by its stated deadline to appear in the next issue. A release that misses the deadline may not appear for another month—too late for your meeting.

Other Options. Depending on your meeting—size, type, and objective—you may do more or less than suggested here to promote the meeting and to secure publicity for your organization before, during, and after the conference. You may, for example, notify editors of journals and newspapers that a press conference will be held during the meeting to make a special announcement or introduce a prominent speaker (it will have to be important to get the press out). Or you may use electronic networks more extensively in promoting the meeting, including electronic mail, Internet advertising, and other forms of computerized publicity.

After the meeting, you may take other steps. For example, you may send another press release to announce important things that happened during the meeting. You may also want to announce the sale of published proceedings to the general public or to interested segments of the public after the meeting.

However, you may not have the available funds or the need for all of the publicity and promotion options described here. Perhaps your meeting has an audience almost guaranteed to attend and meeting-room limitations that prevent you from encouraging greater attendance.

Since every meeting is different, you will have to tailor your publicity and promotion to your own special requirements. But regardless of which options you select, you should conclude your activities for the meeting by undertaking a postmeeting evaluation of your committee's work, writing a final Publicity and Promotion Committee report, and submitting your report to the Planning Committee.

Registration

The Registration Committee. One of the most important forms of attendee contact involves the registration of participants. Consider again the example used in previous chapters: a national organization holding a three-day meeting in Cleveland. This time imagine that you're the chair of the Registration Committee. What are your duties?

Your first step should be to review the description of preliminary steps provided in Chapter 4. This includes selecting one to three people to be on your committee, setting a date for the first committee meeting, and preparing for it by studying the bylaws and other rules, previous meeting materials, and instructions from the Planning Committee.

During this time or soon after, the finance chair will no doubt ask you for a Registration Committee budget. Upon its approval, the chair will tell you what your committee may spend on its own and which items require prior authorization. At the first committee meeting, relay any information you have about budgetary matters. Also, give the members an address list of the other committee chairs and review the meeting theme, objectives, desired audience and attendance, and other key elements.

Be prepared to make committee task assignments. Perhaps one person will be in charge of creating the registration form and working with a printer or desktop publishing department (or with the person who is in charge of printing for the meeting). Another may be in charge of processing incoming registrations. Someone else may be responsible for setting up a registration booth at the conference site and arranging for assistants to operate it.

Program-Registration Package. If the Publicity and Promotion Committee is arranging to print and mail a general program-registration package, your job will be to assist that committee in preparing the portion pertaining to registration. Be prepared to draft the copy concerning when and how to register. Then, design an actual card or sheet that people can fill out and mail in with their checks.

If you don't have a computer program with suitable models, review the material used for previous meetings or ask a printer to show you samples. After you've submitted your draft, the program or publicity chair will get approval of the entire program-registration package from the

Planning Committee and will arrange for the mass mailing.

Registration Fee. The registration fee must be set based on anticipated attendance and overall meeting expenses. A number of people will be involved in the decision-making process. Although the Planning Committee will authorize the final figure, you and the finance chair should be actively involved in this part of the meeting arrangements.

Other committee chairs will also have important information affecting the amount that will have to be charged for registration. The facilities and meals chairs, for example, may have cost figures so high that it will be necessary to charge a higher fee than originally planned.

Perhaps the decision will be to have a varied fee structure, with a low general fee but extra charges for special events, such as a dinner-dance and for a copy of the proceedings. Or you may have one fee that covers everything. Also, members of the organization may have a lower registration fee than the one for nonmembers. Late registrations (after a certain date or at the door) may be higher too—to encourage people to register and pay early.

Another question concerns the method of payment. Will you allow credit cards? Will you accept unpaid registrations and bill people? Will you refund 100 percent on cancellations up to a certain date and less after that date? Will you give group discounts or student discounts? Your organization may have a strict policy about some of these matters.

Once you and the finance chair have submitted your recommendations to the Planning Committee, it will make a final decision. You can then incorporate the information into your draft for the program-registration packet.

Advance Registration. Meetings such as seminars and conferences may have two types of registration: preregistration, or advance registration, and on-site, or door, registration. A prime objective of any registration committee is to get as many people as possible registered—with fees paid—in advance.

A seminar or workshop with established limits on attendance (perhaps registration closes after the first forty registrations) doesn't have the same concerns as a conference. Whereas the conference may be open to as many people as the sponsor can entice to come, the seminar or workshop with limited space only has to reach a certain number, often fewer than a hundred people.

In the case of a large conference open to as many people as the sponsors can find, almost everything hinges on numbers. For example, how many meeting rooms and meals should be ordered—enough for five hundred, a thousand, two thousand? How much should be charged for registration? Presumably, the fee will be less if attendance is two thousand than if it is two hundred.

To make intelligent decisions about reservations and financial matters, one has to have a fairly accurate estimate of attendance. To a certain extent, this estimate is made in the early planning stages based on experience (previous meeting attendance) and projected response to promotional activity. But firm figures are possible only with hard evidence—the receipt of actual registration forms and checks.

Although large conferences nearly always have some on-site, or door, registration, it can be overwhelming to have hundreds of people unexpectedly appear at the door on the opening day of the meeting. Therefore, the goal of the organizers is to get most people registered well in advance of the meeting date.

Numerous questions arise when too many people wait until they arrive to register. Will it still be possible to get additional meeting rooms or larger rooms? Can the hotel suddenly feed, say, four hundred unexpected attendees? Can a printer quickly provide that many extra programs? (One should always do an overrun, however, in case more people show up later.)

Record Keeping. Because so much hinges on attendance, you need to keep accurate records and be able to report changes regularly (daily, in some instances). Although you will likely keep the actual incoming registration forms in an alphabetical file (where new ones can be added and cancellations pulled out), it will be too time-consuming to have someone recount the forms every day—hence the need for continually updated tally sheets and routinely revised computer records.

Have your staff keep a written tally sheet as the mail is opened each day (how many are registered for this or that session and how many in all?) and then enter the figures in your computer records. Also, send updated reports to the Program Committee and the Planning Committee. If there's a meeting coordinator, this person will keep the other key players informed.

Nearly everyone will be watching advance registration returns closely. The finance chair will want to know how income and expenses are running. The Facilities Committee and the Meals and Entertainment Committee will want to know if they've underbooked or overbooked. The Program Committee will be wondering if it needs to add more sessions to accommodate extra attendance or cancel some if attendance is running below estimates.

Your computer records may include a registrant address list, with data such as amount paid, sessions selected, and tickets purchased for special events. This list can be updated right up to the time of leaving for the conference site and can be used at the on-site registration desk as a check-in guide.

Routinely, coordinate your registration-processing activities with the accounting department and the bookkeeper in charge of recording income and expenses. You'll have to turn over receipts to the designated person along with names or other information as required.

Door Registration. During advance registration, as the forms and checks begin to arrive, your office staff will soon be trained in handling the paperwork, computer processing, and telephone inquiries. You will then have to decide whether to transport this staff to the meeting site to run the registration desk there or whether the staff is needed at the home site during the meeting.

If the staff won't be going, you'll need to arrange (through the hotel or a convention bureau) for secretarial services or a trained outside staff to take over during the meeting. Or you may decide to use volunteers from among the membership of your organization.

Certain equipment and supplies, such as computers, fax machines, copiers, and so on, can be secured at the site through the hotel. But other supplies you'll need to transport to the site. Make a list of supplies and records that should be taken to the meeting site and find out what materials other committees will be sending for use or distribution at the registration desk. Your list will likely include these items:

- Diskettes

- Paper and disk files

- Cash lockboxes (arrange to take cash receipts to a bank—don't leave a lot of cash lying around—and put it in a hotel safe if the banks are closed)

- Credit-card processing machines

- Notebooks

- Pens and pencils

- Receipt books

- Badges for registrants (the badges can be typed at the home office as registrations come in; have them in alphabetical order at the on-site registration desk)

- Maps and brochures of the city

- Tickets to special events

- Signs

Some items may be mailed in advance to early registrants. In fact, as registrations arrive, you should immediately mail a confirmation notice to those registrants. This may be a printed card or duplicate copy of the registration form marked "paid." Study the confirmation notices used in previous meetings or ask a printer to show you samples of notices and other registration materials.

On-Site Registration Setup. The hotel will provide a desk, table, or booth for the registration staff. Let the Facilities Committee know what your needs will be and where you want the booth located. Often the registration desk or booth is in a prominent location in a lobby or hallway where attendees will see it immediately on arriving at the portion of the hotel set aside for the meeting. But be certain it doesn't complicate the traffic flow to meeting rooms.

If a registration table is used, arrange for a floor-length table skirt so that you can store supplies beneath it, out of sight. Put signs on poles or in some other visible place to direct people to the table or booth and to specify the place for "Advance Registration Check-In" and "New Registrations," "Name Tags," "Ticket Sales," "Proceedings Sales," and "Press Kits."

In the same area, other committees may set up their own booths, such as a child-care check-in desk or an information booth. All of this activity and placement should be arranged through or coordinated with the Facilities Committee.

Postmeeting Registration Details. Arrange to return all registration records and supplies to the home site after the meeting. Make your final accounting to the bookkeeper or accounting department (although you still may have to bill some unpaid registrations when you return).

When the last registration fee or other receipt is accounted for and your registration list for the meeting is complete, conduct a postmeeting analysis for the use of future committees and make a final report to the Planning Committee. Find out if the registration address list should be turned over to someone in the organization for incorporation into an established database or a mailing list to be used for future conference mailings.

Attendee Problems

Have strategies prepared for dealing with troublesome registrants. Although attendance etiquette requires that registrants be quiet, courteous, and cooperative at a meeting, not everyone has the best possible manners. You may find unruly people—some who are angry that the session they wanted to attend is full—and even thieves. It's not unusual to find that copies of proceedings on sale have disappeared or even that cash boxes are suddenly gone without a trace.

The Planning Committee may appoint someone to remove unruly people (see also Section 67 in the second part of the book on meeting conduct). Otherwise, decide in advance—with the Facilities Committee and the meeting chair—who will handle such problems. (For serious matters, consult an attorney and be certain that you understand your rights and the rights of the attendees.)

In regard to theft, be prepared with good security. Don't hesitate to have a staff member or volunteer from the organization act as a watchdog in the registration area. Establish advance procedures with the hotel security staff (the Facilities Committee may do this) so that you know the person to call if a crime occurs. Have available at all times a number for the local police. Also, have a place, perhaps at the registration site, for people to report lost and found items (the hotel will have such a department too).

Find out in advance from the hotel management or the Facilities Committee the proper procedure for handling emergencies. Ask if there is a house physician or someone else to contact in case an injury or illness that occurs during the meeting is reported at the registration desk.

7. FACILITIES

The Site and Facilities

An organization sometimes has a circuit it travels for meetings. Perhaps a significant percentage of its membership or other interested people are located in various large cities, such as Chicago or Los Angeles. It's almost a necessity, then, to schedule meetings in each of the cities with such large clusters of prospective attendees.

Other organizations may simply choose a city that will appeal to people for other reasons. It may be a wonderful place to visit or an ideal place to which to bring the family for a combined meeting and vacation. The choice of the particular facilities, such as a hotel or convention center, is not always as obvious. A lot can go wrong, in fact, with this part of the meeting arrangements.

The Facilities Committee. Assume, as you did in previous chapters, that you're one of the key meeting arrangers for a national organization holding a three-day meeting in Cleveland. A substantial portion of the organization's membership and prospective audience is there, and the organization hasn't met in Cleveland for five years, so it's time to return.

Your assignment for this meeting is to chair the Facilities Committee. Specifically, you will be concerned with selecting the best hotel, convention center, university, town hall, or other place to hold the three-day event. After the facility is chosen, you'll be concerned with details such as how many rooms are needed, what size they must be, and what they will cost.

The Planning Committee may have indicated its facilities preference for the meeting but may want you to make other suggestions. Your first task, then, is to form a committee and set a date for a meeting.

Follow the preliminary steps given in Chapter 4. Review the bylaws and rules of the organization, find out what the Planning Committee wants, and prepare a committee-chair address list and summary of key meeting objectives to give to your committee members. Have a preliminary meeting schedule prepared and be certain that the committee members know the various deadlines.

Check whether there are any checklists or other forms in a computer program or on file from previous meetings that you can use. If not, look for samples in a conference planning guide or devise your own.

Investigation of Facilities. Assign tasks to your committee members at the first committee meeting. Initially, everyone may be assigned one or more facilities in the city to investigate (to visit, collect literature about, and determine general suitability).

After that, one person may be in charge of arrangements for the meeting rooms. Someone else may handle the rooms for meals or entertainment. Another person may see about airport transportation to the hotel for out-of-town attendees.

Make a list of things that you want each committee member to find out concerning the prospective facilities. Since the appropriate facilities should be visited in person (a telephone call or letter won't do for serious possibilities), it will help to have local residents on the committee.

Once you have compiled a detailed list of things your organization will need from a facility, your committee is ready to start investigating facilities. Arrange to meet again, as soon as possible, with everyone bringing enough information for you to select the best facility. Then submit your recommendation to the Planning Committee for final approval.

Selection of Facilities. After a thorough investigation of prospective sites and facilities, your committee may have concluded that the New Hotel in downtown Cleveland has the most appropriate facilities for your meeting.

Perhaps the Planning Committee agrees for these reasons:

- The hotel's prices are competitive.

- It has a reputation for excellent service.

- It is a modern facility, and the shopping and entertainment available in the downtown area are appealing, especially for attendees who bring along their spouses and children.

- Plenty of parking is available in a new underground parking lot, and there are more than adequate blocks of sleeping rooms.

- The meeting-room layouts, lighting, temperature, and furniture are perfect.

- There are modern fax and computer services as well as private-room hookups.

- The hotel has ramps, elevators, and other features to accommodate persons with disabilities.

- It has a good paging system, active lost and found department, and clear directional signs on each floor.

- You believe that the hotel staff will be very cooperative and will give your organization an abundance of assistance while you're making the arrangements and will help to ensure that all goes smoothly during the meeting.

Everyone agrees that the New Hotel is an excellent choice, but this doesn't mean that you can relax. A facilities committee usually has an exceptionally heavy work load, and this is only the beginning for you and your committee members.

The finance chair may already be waiting for a committee budget from you, so you should prepare one as soon as possible. The Program Committee may also be waiting for facilities information to put in the program-registration packet. Other committees also will be waiting for facilities information.

Hotel Costs. The hotel, meanwhile, will have named a representative to work with you not only in selecting the physical accommodations but in establishing the related costs. But don't accept the first prices that are mentioned for the various facilities and services you need. Find out the usual rates for the things you need and negotiate the best price for your organization.

If this is the first meeting of your organization at this hotel, you may have to make a deposit (the final bill will be payable after the event). Arrange to make the deposit after a certain percentage of paid registrations has arrived. If your organization has met at this hotel before and has established credit with the hotel, the payment schedule may be more flexible.

It's common, however, for hotels to ask for certain commitments concerning attendance. Be prepared, therefore, to have to guarantee in writing the number of participants for certain events. If your attendance falls short, you will still have to pay the agreed-upon amount. (Work with the Planning Committee and the Registration Committee in evaluating expected attendance.)

The Contract. Hotels have their own contracts or agreements, but your organization also may have its own contracts for services at a facility (the hotel may insist on using its own, however). Either way, read the contract(s) carefully and be certain that everything you expect to receive is listed.

Items to be listed include not only the service but the associated costs. There should also be a clarification of things the hotel will do and the things your organization will do, as well as the deadlines or times that these things will be provided.

Do not use a facility that refuses to state all services and costs in the contract. If something isn't specified, you may not get it later or at least not at the price you expected. Once you're satisfied with the terms, give a copy of the contract(s) to the Planning Committee for it to study (the meeting chair usually signs contracts for the meeting).

Supplies and Accommodations. By now you no doubt have submitted a facilities budget to the finance chair

and have received approval, with an indication of what
you may spend or contract for on your own, without
prior authorization, and what must first be approved. It's
time, then, to move immediately toward arrangements
for the supplies and accommodations that you'll need.
You'll also need some of this information in order to
determine what to have listed in the contract(s).

Ask each committee to send you a detailed list of its
requirements (a meeting coordinator is very helpful in
making such contacts with other committees). Ask the
Program Committee to send you a list of speaker requirements. Also request a list from the Registration
Committee or any other person or committee that needs
rooms, supplies, equipment, or anything else at the
meeting pertaining to the facilities.

Depending on the complexity of the meeting, you could
handle the detailed arrangements in various ways. But in
all meetings, it's important to have separate lists of requirements for items such as the following:

- Supplies (including working supplies for the staff
  and speakers)

- Rooms (for registration, meeting, sleeping, eating,
  entertaining)

- Meals and refreshments

- Social events

- Exhibits and displays

- Equipment for speakers (audiovisual aids, copy
  boards, and so on)

- Fax, computer, and other equipment for the meeting arrangers and their staffs

- Wheelchairs and other aids for disabled persons

- On-site secretarial, registration, and other personnel

- Signs

- Transportation (of materials, participants, and
  speakers) to and from airports and other locations

The hotel representative will need a copy of each list, as will the Planning Committee and the meeting coordinator. Each committee will need a copy of the list pertaining to its own function.

By now you will have written instructions from the hotel concerning what you may and may not do. This will affect where you set up booths, where you sell publications and other items, where you put up signs, and so on. You will also soon know which items on your various lists you must provide and which the hotel will provide.

Make new lists of the supplies, equipment, personnel, and other things that you must provide. Contact the appropriate people in your organization to determine what is in stock and what must be ordered. Place any necessary orders and reservations immediately.

Room Setup. Begin working on the physical layout and room-setup requirements. The hotel will let you know about any labor requirements, such as who may take care of cables, electrical needs, and so on.

The Program Committee can give you a schedule of speakers and room-setup requirements for each one, including handout material, equipment, and supplies. Make committee and on-site staff assignments to handle the arrival and distribution of the various materials and equipment at the appropriate times.

Be certain that reservations for materials and other orders have all been placed and follow up before the meeting to ensure that everything has arrived or will be arriving on time. Arrange for the transportation of any materials that won't be delivered by a supplier to the hotel. (See the discussions of equipment and presentation aids and exhibits and demonstrations later in this chapter.)

On-Site Duties. Although a large committee or staff can be unwieldy without strong supervision and coordination, there is so much to do with facilities arrangements that it helps to have enough assistants available so that no person is overwhelmed with too much work. Sometimes it's easier if one person can focus exclusively on a single item or a few related items.

One person, for example, may be concerned only with

supplies, equipment, and presentation aids for speakers. Someone else may be concerned exclusively with transportation needs. Another person may handle room setup (such as theater style, with everyone facing the front; classroom style, with rectangular tables and people facing the front; or conference-banquet style, with round or horseshoe tables and people facing each other). Other assistants will similarly handle other tasks.

Throughout all of this activity, maintain open communications with the meeting coordinator and other committees, such as the Registration Committee and the Meals and Entertainment Committee. Their needs may change, and you in turn may have to make adjustments in the arrangements for room setup. Be certain to notify the finance chair immediately if any changes cause your budget to be revised.

At the site, during the meeting, maintain an ongoing check of the facilities, supplies, and other items. Be certain that the various people assigned to the different tasks monitor their activities properly throughout the meeting and afterward.

Even after the meeting has ended, numerous tasks still have to be handled. For example, all of the things that were ordered and transported to the site have to be returned. Bills have to be reviewed and forwarded for payment. Finally, after the last step has been taken in regard to materials and finances, a postmeeting evaluation should be conducted and a detailed report on your facilities activities prepared for the Planning Committee.

Meals and Entertainment

Many organizations serve lunch, dinner, or morning or afternoon refreshments (or all of these things) during a meeting. Sometimes such meetings are held in a company conference room and the participants adjourn to the company dining room for the meal. Or snacks and beverages may be catered to the meeting room or an adjacent area in the morning or afternoon.

Many meetings, however, are held in a hotel or motel,

sometimes near a major airport if some of the participants come from out of town. In that case, one usually selects a menu and arranges with the facility to seat a certain number during the meal. Sometimes the food and beverages are brought into the meeting room by the hotel or motel catering service or restaurant personnel.

Meals and Entertainment Committee. The arrangements for meals and snacks become more complicated when you're making plans for a longer meeting, particularly one that runs two or more days. Although the Facilities Committee may handle food and beverage arrangements, sometimes there is a separate meals or meals and entertainment committee.

Assume that you're the chair of such a committee for a national organization preparing to hold a three-day meeting in Cleveland. Like all other chairs, you'll start by reviewing instructions from the Planning Committee, preliminary information about the proposed meeting, and the organization's bylaws and other rules. You'll then select one to three people to serve on your committee and set up a first meeting.

At the first meeting you'll want to explain the purpose and objectives of the three-day event and brief your committee members on instructions, organization policy, deadlines, and the procedure followed by previous meals and entertainment committees. You should also give everyone an address list of the other committees chairs and make work assignments. Before adjourning, set a date for the next committee meeting. (See Chapter 4 for an outline of preliminary committee procedures.)

Coordination with Other Committees. Providing information to other committees is a top priority. To begin, the Finance Committee will need a meals and entertainment budget from you as soon as possible. After it has been approved, the finance chair will let you know what you may spend on your own and what will require prior authorization.

Other committees also will be waiting for information from you. The Registration Committee, for example, has to consider meals and entertainment details when writing the copy for the registration form and when arranging for tickets to be used for special functions. The cost of food and beverages, as well as the cost of entertainment functions, also figures in the price of registration for the meeting.

The Program Committee needs details on food and beverages and on entertainment to add to the instructions that will be part of the program-registration mailer. It also needs to list any cocktail party, banquet, or other special event on the program.

Meals and Entertainment Requirements. The Planning Committee may instruct you concerning how many meals are desired, or you may be asked to recommend such things and provide the schedule. Either way, since you'll be working closely with the Planning Committee and the Facilities Committee, as well as with other committees, a meeting coordinator will be very helpful in maintaining open communication with all of the key arrangers.

In regard to the major meals, assume that everyone wants to provide—as part of the registration fee—three lunches, one dinner, and one cocktail party (preceding dinner) with a small musical group or perhaps just a piano player. Members and their families may, in addition, purchase tickets for a tour of the cultural sites in the city (perhaps one tour each afternoon). How do you arrange all of this?

Contact the hotel representative assigned to work with the Facilities Committee (he or she may contact you) and arrange a meeting, preferably including the facilities chair since meals also require rooms—the responsibility of the Facilities Committee. Explain to the hotel representative what your organization wants and ask what the hotel has to offer to accommodate those needs.

The hotel will want you to give an attendance guarantee for all meals probably forty-eight hours in advance of each event. You then have to pay for the number you guarantee even if fewer registrants appear. A hotel can usually accommodate up to 10 percent more than your estimate, and you should ask the Facilities Committee to arrange for rooms of adequate size in case attendance increases unexpectedly at the last minute.

The meeting chair usually signs all contracts, including

any for meals and entertainment. But before contracts are prepared, be certain to submit your meals and entertainment plans and schedule to the Planning Committee for approval. Also, discuss with the Facilities Committee the type of room settings (such as banquet style) and lighting that are needed for each particular meal or event.

Menu Selection. Selecting the menus for the three lunches and the one dinner should be a joint activity. Let the hotel representative know that you'd like to see a choice of menus and listen to the advice of others on your own committee and on the Facilities Committee. For example, perhaps someone will point out ethnic or other considerations in the choice of foods and beverages. Also decide what other meals you want to offer (such as breakfast for a board of directors' meeting).

In general, lunches should be lighter than dinners, and the meat should be different for each meal (attendees would grow weary of chicken every day). Remember to consider the needs of an increasing number of vegetarians in your planning. Avoid the "vegetable of the day" type of menu since then you don't know what you're getting until the meal is served. Also, keep in mind that exotic meals involving a lot of distraction while being served are a poor choice when there will be a guest lunch or dinner speaker.

Alcohol is not recommended for meals—registrants want to stay awake during the sessions—although a cocktail party or cash bar is common before dinner (it closes, then, in one to two hours). This type of event should include nonalcoholic beverages.

Refreshment Breaks. Your organization may decide to provide morning and afternoon refreshment breaks in addition to the meals. Refreshment breaks, which may be set up in meeting rooms or in hallways (if they don't interrupt traffic flow), or the registration lobby, usually consist of coffee and other beverages, such as fruit juice or soft drinks. Snacks may include doughnuts, rolls, cookies, granola bars, or sherbert.

Although some groups try to economize by skipping breaks, this is usually counterproductive. Most attendees need to refresh themselves to avoid attention loss and fatigue during the many sessions they attend throughout the day.

Costs. Ask the hotel representative to clarify all costs. Find out if the prices include gratuities and taxes. If everything is more than your budget can accommodate, ask the hotel representative to suggest subtle economies. During breaks, for example, a glass full of chilled beverage alone costs more than a glass that's half beverage and half crushed ice.

Once you have menus that you like and prices that you can afford, be certain it's all guaranteed in the contract. Don't take a chance that prices will be the same by the time the meeting arrives.

Tickets. Tickets are usually printed for special events, such as a banquet or tour, especially when the price is not included in the registration fee. The Registration Committee may handle part or all of such arrangements, such as the printing, but you should work closely with the chair on all such matters.

If music or other entertainment is to be provided at a cocktail party or one of the meals, arrangements can usually be made through the hotel. Organizations also may contract on their own with outside musicians (consistent with hotel regulations for entertainment on the premises).

Tours, too, are commonly arranged through the hotel. Also, large facilities regularly help visitors secure theater tickets, passes to sporting events, and entry to other special events, whether or not they are part of the meeting program.

The advance-registration material should announce special events and provide a place for registrants to make reservations. Tickets also are commonly sold in the registration area. If no more space is available for a particular event, a Sold Out notice should be posted and alternatives suggested to interested persons.

Coordinate all of the preceding arrangements closely with the Registration Committee, the Program Committee, and the Facilities Committee. In addition, report arrangements regularly to the Planning Committee.

On-Site Duties. During the meeting, monitor attendance carefully so that you know if your estimates for the meals are correct. Other members of your committee should participate in all of these matters.

You may, in fact, designate one person to be in charge of lunches, another in charge of dinner and the refreshment breaks, and someone else in charge of the special events, such as tours. Ask each person to report regularly to you so that you can inform the finance chair immediately if the numbers—and costs—change at any time before or during the meeting.

After the meeting, make your final contact with the hotel representative; review all food, beverage, and entertainment bills for accuracy; and forward the bills to the designated person for approval and payment. Then undertake a postmeeting evaluation of the meals and entertainment function and submit a final report to the Planning Committee.

Equipment and Presentation Aids

Someone addressing a local club at lunch might talk for twenty-five minutes without using any equipment or other presentation aids except for a podium and a microphone. But a speaker at a seminar or conference would likely want at least some type of presentation board and a pointer and possibly some type of projector or audio or video equipment.

The task for the people in charge of equipment and presentation aids—often the Facilities and Program committees—is to find out what a speaker needs for his or her presentation and to order it and have it set up in the room where the person will be speaking. (See Chapter 5 and the information on room setup in this chapter.)

The Program Committee makes the first contact with a speaker and therefore is the logical committee to determine what equipment and presentation aids the speaker needs. A common procedure is to enclose an equipment checklist with each speaker's confirmation letter (the letter sent after a speaker accepts an invitation to speak). The speaker can then check off each item that he or she wants and return the list to the program chair (the person who writes the confirmation letter).

With a large meeting, such as the three-day meeting in Cleveland described in previous chapters, the arrangements for equipment and presentation aids can be extensive. There may be thirty or more speakers, all wanting different equipment and presentation aids set up at different times in different rooms.

Not only must one place numerous orders, but the Facilities Committee must also be certain that the equipment and presentation aids are delivered to the site and set up—in proper working order—before the speaker and audience arrive. Sometimes equipment must be changed in the brief period between sessions as one group is exiting and before the next group enters.

Equipment Availability. Some of the equipment and presentation aids will be available through the hotel; some things your organization may have in stock; other items will have to be ordered from suppliers at the site. The hotel or local residents on the Facilities Committee can probably suggest places to contact.

Costs. Anything the hotel can provide that is suitable and for which the rental charge is within your budget should be considered. If it's already at the site, you will avoid transportation costs and potential problems. Even if it isn't already at the site, the hotel will take care of the ordering and follow-up as well as delivery. However, you should monitor this activity even if the hotel assumes responsibility for it.

If the hotel's charge for taking care of securing the equipment and presentation aids is too high and you want to order from outside suppliers yourself, be certain to check whether the hotel will allow you to bring in the equipment in question. Regardless of your decision, anything the hotel is going to provide and the cost should be listed in the written contract.

Some items, such as presentation boards, erasers, and podiums, are usually provided free by the hotel. Ask the hotel representative what is free and what must be rented. The contract should list and specify "no charge" for the free items.

Equipment Checklist. Your organization may have a standard checklist that speakers and others can use for requesting equipment and presentation aids. Or you may find a suitable checklist in a computer program. If none is available, devise one yourself that lists everything a speaker may need for the meeting. It should include the following general items and anything else pertinent to your particular meeting. (See also the discussion of a speaker data form in Chapter 5.)

- Projectors (overhead, 8 mm, 16 mm, 35 mm, film-strip, and so on)
- Screens (for projectors) and required sizes
- Microphones (floor, podium, clip-on, and so on)
- PA system
- Recorders (such as cassette) and blank tapes
- Computers and accessories
- Video equipment and accessories
- Boards (electronic copy boards, chalkboards, chart-boards, bulletin boards, and so on), easels, pads, and miscellaneous supplies (pointers, marking pens, and so on)
- Lighting and other electrical needs (receptacles, adapters, remote controls, and so on)
- Podiums (standing, tabletop, and so on), amplification system, and gavels

Make your checklist as detailed as possible. But also assume that some speaker will want something that isn't on your list and include numerous "other" lines for this purpose: ( ) Other_____.

Sometimes a speaker prefers to bring his or her own equipment or presentation aids. Include a place on your checklist for the speaker to list such items (and to check who pays for the rental).

On-Site Setup. Setting up equipment and presentation aids for numerous speakers (as well as setting up the rooms with tables, pencils, pads, fresh water, and other things for the attendees) is too much of a task for one person. The Facilities Committee, working with the Program Committee, should divide the labor among the various committee members, staff assistants, and volunteers from the organization sponsoring the meeting.

Time is crucial in the actual setup process, so workers should be thoroughly briefed and given schedules broken down into minutes. When hotel or other outside services are involved in the setup (often this is a requirement), be certain you understand any labor union rules and regulations.

Be prepared for emergencies. Although a piece of equipment should be tested before the speaker uses it, and it should not be assumed that everything is working properly, the equipment still could fail during a presentation. What will you do?

Have emergency strategies written out for everyone, especially an indication of where backup equipment can be secured immediately. Develop your backup strategies in cooperation with the hotel representative so that everyone clearly understands what can and should be done if such emergencies occur.

After the meeting, ensure that everything is dismantled and returned to the proper source. Then collect and review all rental bills and forward them to the appropriate person for payment. When the last task is finished, conduct a postmeeting analysis of the equipment and presentation aids arrangements and submit a final report to the Planning Committee.

Exhibits and Demonstrations

Organizations whose members deal in products that can be displayed or demonstrated at a meeting may want to hold a trade show or incorporate exhibits into the program of a conference. Using the example from previous chapters, a national organization holding a three-day conference in Cleveland might want to allocate space for members and others to display and demonstrate their products.

Such displays may consist only of printed material and photographs, or they may include products and equipment. If the Planning Committee wants something more extensive than just a few booths with literature handouts, it should appoint an Exhibits Committee to handle these arrangements (or the Facilities Committee may do it).

The Exhibits Committee. Assume that you've just been appointed exhibits chair. Follow the preliminary steps outlined in Chapter 4. Review instructions from the Planning Committee, study the bylaws and other rules, and select one to three people for your committee.

Set up a committee meeting as soon as possible and brief the members on the objectives, schedules, and other details of the upcoming meeting. Give each member an address list of other committee chairs and describe procedures established by previous exhibits committees.

Make task assignments. For example, someone may work with the Facilities Committee in regard to space requirements (perhaps you want display areas of ten-by-ten feet each). Another member may handle arrangements for materials the exhibitors will need (tables, wall boards, and so on). Someone else may handle arrangements for the physical installation, operation, and removal of the exhibits.

Exhibitors. You will be busy, at least initially, with a variety of duties. One of your first tasks will be to develop a list of prospective exhibitors. Compile a list from former conference exhibitors and attendees, trade journals, membership directories, the Yellow Pages, and other likely sources of prospects.

As soon as possible, prepare an exhibits budget for the finance chair. He or she will let you know what is approved and what expenditures you may incur with or without prior authorization. Also work with the Planning Committee in developing exhibit and display rules and regulations—hours that exhibits will be open, type of materials that will be allowed, type of demonstrations that will be allowed, rental fees for display space, and so on.

Select exhibitors that will enhance the overall meeting program. Products and equipment displayed should be reliable and reputable. For example, you wouldn't want to allow someone to display a product that you have learned is on the verge of being banned as a health hazard.

You or the facilities chair will need to confirm with the hotel representative which items exhibitors may or may not bring on the premises. You also need to know the associated hotel charges for various items (additional electrical needs, special labor setup requirements, and so on) as well as the overall cost of holding the show.

Meanwhile, the Publicity and Promotion Committee will be waiting for details about the exhibitors and the displays to include in its publicity announcements. The Program and Registration committees will need details for the advance program-registration mailer. (A meeting coordinator will be very helpful in maintaining the necessary contacts with other committees.) When details are firm, you should contact the exhibitors you've selected from your prospect list.

Exhibit Requirements. The displays will have certain space, electrical, and other requirements. Often exhibits are set up in one or more rooms that can be divided by curtains or partitions into numerous individual areas.

The hotel may offer a setup service, but if its fee is too high, you may want to check the Yellow Pages for a firm that provides trade-show services at a more reasonable cost. Some organizations will do everything— contact the prospective exhibitors, book the space, contract with the hotel, and, in general, run the entire show.

If you don't want the hotel or an outside firm to set up the show—or if your budget won't permit this—you will need a good team of volunteers to assist you in handling it yourself. In that case, find out what the hotel or convention center will permit you to handle on your own.

Devise or secure an already prepared floor plan for the displays as soon as you know what space will be available. If the show is going to be very large, you'll probably be meeting in a convention center with a huge showroom and specially designed places for exhibits. A large facility that commonly holds trade shows will have a basic floor plan for you to work with.

If a basic plan is not available, however, use your computer and the appropriate graphics or other program to prepare a scale floor plan. Number the individual exhibit areas—perhaps you plan to have fifty exhibits. Exhibitors, then, can be assigned numbered display areas when they want to reserve space. Include aisles and entry and exit doorways on your drawing so that you can visualize traffic flow.

Exhibitor Contacts. The first letter to prospective exhibitors should do the following:

- Introduce your organization

- Describe the upcoming meeting

- Profile the expected exhibits

- Provide a timetable or schedule for the displays

- Give the prospects a good reason for exhibiting their products or equipment

Include a reply card with this first letter so that interested parties can ask for more information with minimal effort.

The next contact—a follow-up mailing to the best prospects, including those who sent back reply cards—should include more information about the exhibits, including the following:

- A copy of your floor plan

- Details on rental charges for exhibit spaces

- Specific program information

- Essential facts about the facility

- Information on security

- Transportation and shipping requirements

- A clear statement about the type of equipment and products that are desired and permitted for display

- Delivery times and places

- A copy of the contract that exhibitors must sign

Exhibitor Contract. Include lines on the exhibitor contract for the exhibitors to specify pertinent details: the type of display they will have (with a list of associated products, equipment, supplies, and so on), any physical requirements (tables, chairs, special lighting, electrical needs, and so on), and the space desired (selected from your numbered floor plan), with second and third choices.

If you'll be providing the signs, have a space on the contract for the exhibitors to specify the desired wording for their exhibit signs. If you're going to provide name tags apart from those prepared by the Registration Committee for attendees, ask the exhibitors to specify the names, job titles, and company affiliations for all who will need name tags at the exhibits.

The Planning Committee may have a standard contract for exhibitors at its conferences or for those at separate trade shows. If you must draft a new contract, submit it to the Planning Committee for approval (the meeting chair usually signs all contracts).

On-Site Duties. Assign on-site duties to members of your committee, your office staff, and volunteers from your organization. If you don't want the hotel or a trade-show service to set up the display area, find out if you are permitted to handle this on your own. Then brief your crew of assistants and volunteers and be ready to prepare the exhibit spaces before the conference opens.

Assign some volunteers to welcome and register exhibitors and to welcome and direct viewers when the display area opens. One or more persons also should serve as contacts for the exhibitors with needs and problems. (Set up an information desk for this purpose). Throughout the arrangements process and during the show, remember to keep the Planning Committee and other concerned persons (such as the finance chair) informed.

After the exhibits close, be certain that everything is dismantled as required and returned to the proper source. Then collect and review final bills, forwarding them to the designated person for payment. Prepare a list of registered exhibitors (for future meetings), undertake a postmeeting evaluation of the exhibits and demonstrations function, and make a final report to the Planning Committee.

8. MEETING RECORDS

The Minutes

The meeting *minutes,* the most common type of meeting record, is a record of the business transacted at a meeting, such as the business discussed at a board of directors' meeting. The minutes may not be formally published. The *proceedings* are a published collection of the papers presented by speakers at a larger meeting, such as a seminar or conference.

The Recorder. The recording officer of an organization, known as the clerk or secretary, is the official minute taker in a formal meeting. (See Sections 41 and 51 in the second part of this book on meeting conduct for proper recording procedure under the rules of parliamentary law.) In many small, informal meetings, however, someone else, such as an office secretary, may do the actual note taking.

In addition, tape recorders are commonly used to make an audio backup. In very large meetings, a videotape of the proceedings may also be made. But someone should always take notes in case of tape or equipment failure.

Regardless of who actually takes the notes, and regardless of how informal a meeting may be, it's important to have an accurate record of what was said and agreed to by the participants. With the exception of casual office or social conversations, notes should always be prepared by typewriter or computer in an organized form. The bylaws of an organization should indicate any requirements in this respect.

The person doing the recording should arrive before

the meeting begins to assemble his or her equipment, materials, and supplies for both manual note taking and for audio or video recording. The supplies should include a notebook, copy of the agenda, fill-in forms for easy recording of motions and resolutions, reference material on topics to be discussed or reported at the meeting, pencils and pens, seating chart, and so on.

A recording secretary who is also an officer of the organization should sit next to the chair. An office secretary or outside recorder will likely sit nearby in a position from which it is possible to see all speakers during the meeting.

If you're doing the recording and don't know everyone, make a seating chart, with the help of the chair or someone else, so that you can recognize people who are speaking. If there are too many people for this, ask the chair to instruct the attendees to identify themselves when they speak.

Recording Procedure. Even in a very formal meeting, the recorder usually doesn't attempt to write down every word that's said. In most cases, the objective is to record essential facts (and to do so objectively) or the gist of conversations. For example:

Messrs. Fontana and Sloane and Ms. Racemic discussed the benefits of the new zoning law for service industries.

Resolutions, however, should be recorded in full, including the names of those who made or seconded a motion. You may want to devise a fill-in type of form for recording such material. In any case, record the following facts.

- Wording of the motion

- Who made it

- Who seconded it

- The number voting for (in favor of) it

- The number voting against it

- The number of abstentions

A resolution normally begins with the word *resolved* (sometimes with *whereas*), often followed by the word *that* after *resolved*:

RESOLVED That . . .

Write *RESOLVED* and *WHEREAS* in all capital letters. use an initial capital for *That* when it follows *RESOLVED*. Capitalize *Board of Directors* and *Corporation*. Write amounts of money as words with the numbers in parentheses afterward:

Two Hundred Dollars ($200)

If you're unsure about something, ask the chair or someone else about it during the next break or just before you leave the meeting—definitely before you transcribe your notes. Also, note all times, such as the time of the call to order and the time of adjournment, as well as any other factual data concerning the order of business.

You may have a copy of some material presented at the meeting, such as a treasurer's report, but take notes anyway. Perhaps the copy has been revised and the treasurer is reporting new facts and figures at the meeting.

Transcribing Procedure. Transcribe your notes as soon as possible after the meeting while it's all still fresh in your mind. If you taped the activity, listen to the oral version or watch the video version, comparing it with your written notes.

Minutes are usually prepared by computer and stored in the computer's minutes file. However, paper copies are also placed in a minute folder or book along with copies of reports presented at the meeting.

Format. Use other prepared minutes of previous meetings as a guide to setup. If a sample is unavailable, develop your own format. You may, for example, center the heading, which should include the organization's name, type of meeting, and date.

**The Fine Company
Board of Directors
Regular Monthly Directors Meeting
June 7, 19XX**

In the first paragraph of the minutes, repeat the date and state the place the meeting was held, name of the presiding officer, type of meeting (such as annual, regular, special, and so on), whether a quorum was present, and the time that the meeting was called to order.

Use subheads for individual topics in the body of the minutes (often you can use each item on the agenda as a separate heading). These subheads may be in a left column, with the associated text in an adjacent right column. Or each subhead may appear on a line alone above the associated text paragraphs. For a small meeting, list the names of attendees under the first paragraph. For a very large meeting, state only the number who attended.

CALL TO ORDER

The regular monthly meeting of the Board of Directors of the Fine Company was called to order at 10:00 a.m., Monday, June 7, 19XX, in the Conference Room at 1276 First Avenue. The presiding officer was Wanda Musgrove. A quorum was present, including the following:

[list alphabetically]

Absent were John Wyatt and Susan Moss.

If the minutes are brief, double-space the body and triple-space between each item. Single-space resolutions. If the minutes are very long, single-space them, with a double-space between paragraphs and with extra space above and below each subhead.

When side subheads are used, it's not necessary to indent the paragraphs. When above-text subheads are used, as in the previous example, indent the paragraphs about 1 inch and indent all lines of a resolution about 1½ inches.

At the end—after the last paragraph (headed "Adjournment")—add two lines for the secretary (on the left) and the presiding officer (on the right) to write their signatures. (Sometimes only the secretary of the organization signs the minutes.)

[handwritten signature]   [handwritten signature]

Secretary   Presiding Officer

Index. The minutes should be indexed so that topics can be located quickly at any time, especially during future meetings. Store the index in your computer and print a revised version after each new set of minutes is filed.

The information for each topic should include the subject and date of the minutes and the book (if any) or computer file as well as the page where the topic can be found. Every time the same subject comes up, add the new date and place it beneath the previous one.

**Zoning: June 7, 19XX, Book 4, page 27
          September 5, 19XX, Book 4, page 51**

Corrections. The minutes may be corrected at future meetings. Changes should be dated in and a revised copy printed. On any revised printout, include a signature line for the secretary and, if desired, another for the presiding officer, the same as you did at the bottom of the original version.

Although it is preferable to have a new printout of revised minutes, you can also make minor changes on a double-spaced printed copy by drawing a line through the incorrect words and writing the correct words above them. In the margin, then, next to the correction, also write the date of the meeting when the minutes were corrected (not the date you correct the copy).

The Proceedings

Copies of a paper presented at a large meeting, such as a seminar or conference, may be distributed by the speaker to the attendees in the room. Some organizations, however, prefer to publish a book containing all or most of the papers presented at a conference. Such collections are commonly called *proceedings*.

A free copy of the proceedings may be given to each registrant as part of the registration fee, or copies may be placed on sale at the meeting (sometimes organizations mail free copies to their members).

Often an organization will print extra copies of the proceedings and, during and after the meeting, promote and sell the books. By doing this, it may be able to recover some of the production costs, possibly earn a profit, and, in any case, at least fulfill its role of disseminating information to an interested public.

Collection of Papers. Assume that for the three-day meeting in Cleveland described in previous chapters you're in charge of the printed proceedings. Perhaps you're a member of the Program Committee, or perhaps the Planning Committee thinks that members of the Program Committee have enough to do and that someone else should be in charge of the proceedings. However, since the Program Committee is developing the program and selecting the speakers, it will no doubt also solicit any desired written or disk copies of each speaker's address.

Papers that are collected will be turned over to you after the Program Committee has verified that they fulfill the requirements of the assigned topic and meet the specifications (length, style, and so on) initially provided by the committee to speakers. (The committee may ask you to develop a set of manuscript- and disk-preparation instructions that can be sent to each speaker.)

Collecting the papers will conclude the Program Committee's active role in the production of the book of proceedings if you have been assigned the task of supervising production. But you'll still want to maintain close contact with the committee in case there are changes in

the program and hence in the papers. It may be too late
to put a last-minute paper in the book, but you still may
want to produce the paper in the same style as the others
and use it as a separate handout at the meeting.

Type of Proccedings. What if the Planning Committee
has not yet given you instructions concerning the type
of proceedings desired, and what if there are no examples from previous years to use as a guide? Ask the
committee if it has any requirements before you contact
various production services for quotes.

Some organizations want their proceedings to look
like any other professionally produced bound book that
you might see in a bookstore. Many organizations, however, prefer a more economical route, which may mean
duplicating the papers exactly as they arrive from the
speakers—errors and all—and either using them as individual handouts at the conference or assembling them
together in some form, such as in an inexpensive binder.

The economical route is also the easiest course for
you. In that case, you don't have to edit and proofread
the papers or arrange for them to be typeset and printed.
The speakers will presumably take care of such matters
before they submit the individual papers.

Production Options. If the papers must be typeset and
printed, however, one of the meeting arrangers may
work for a company that has a desktop publishing department. It may, then, volunteer its services to provide
professionally set pages ready for printing. If it has in-
house printing facilities, it may also provide the printed
copies free of charge or at minimal cost. But if in-house
desktop publishing is not available to you, you will have
to use outside commercial services.

Assume that everyone has decided on a professionally
prepared book of papers. Each paper must then be edited for style and consistency and made to look like a
chapter in a book. The editing, proofreading, and so on
are tasks that you can do on a volunteer basis. But the
typesetting and printing may have to be done by an outside service.

Cost Factors. After talking to the finance chair, you may have doubts that your organization can afford a handsome—but expensive—typeset product within your budget limits. The only way to find out what you can do is to visit several printers, describe your proposed project in detail, and get quotes.

All of the quotes you receive may be similar, but one is usually lower than the others. There are other considerations, though. Does the printer have book-production experience? Have you seen samples of its work? Does it have a reputation for meeting deadlines?

After you've considered all factors, select the firm that you believe can do the best job (it may not have the lowest cost) and submit your recommendation to the finance chair and the Planning Committee.

Once this preliminary work is finished and you have authorization to proceed, be certain that the printer you select has clarified everything in writing. The printer's bid should state everything that will be supplied, along with associated costs (such as delivery to the conference site) according to your timetable.

If you work with an in-house desktop publishing department, find out what it is equipped to handle. If you work with an outside firm, ask about the economies of size. Some sizes of books, for example, involve a lot of paper waste, which also means wasted money.

Information the Printer Needs. Give the printer detailed information about what you will be providing, such as fourteen double-spaced, typed, and edited chapter manuscripts, each averaging 20 pages, for a total of 280 letter-size manuscript pages. Specify how many front-matter and back-matter pages there will be.

The front matter may include a half-title page, title page, copyright page, preface written by the program chair or conference chair, acknowledgments page, and table of contents. The back-matter pages may include a glossary and a subject index. For ideas on setting up front- and back-matter pages, look at the front and back pages of already published books.

Time is often so short that many organizations omit the glossary and index. But the front matter will take less time to prepare, and it's essential if you want the proceedings to look like an actual book. Also, the Planning Committee may have instructed you to copyright the book, so you may want a copyright page at the front in any case. (Call or write to the Library of Congress in Washington, D.C., for current information on the procedure for copyrighting a book.)

Let the printer know how many photographs and how many diagrams, charts, and other line drawings you expect to include. If the book is to be published in black and white only, be certain that the Program Committee has asked speakers to submit eight-by-ten-inch black-and-white glossy photographs and black-and-white computer-generated or other line drawings.

Finally, describe to the printer how you want to handle proofreading. You will presumably want to see proofs of the set pages as well as negative or press proofs that show the position of tables, photographs, and other elements.

Explain that you have a very tight schedule that absolutely must be met. (State the deadline in your contract with the printer.) You won't be able to postpone the meeting to wait for the printer. The completed books *must* be delivered to the conference site on or before the day preceding the opening (ask the Facilities Committee about a preferred delivery date), or you will lose the opportunity to sell copies at the meeting. The printer, therefore, must guarantee completion and delivery in writing.

Style. The organization sponsoring the meeting may have its own preferred style of punctuation, capitalization, spelling, and so on for its books. Or it may always use a standard style book for all of its written and printed material.

If you are expected to choose a style for the proceedings, use a guide that is appropriate for your field. The *Council of Biology Editors Style Manual,* for example, is appropriate for certain scientific works. The *Prentice Hall Style Manual* is appropriate for business material, and the *Chicago Manual of Style* is often used for scholarly or general works.

Edit all papers to be consistent with the style you have chosen. If you are uncertain how to edit a manuscript, find an example to follow. Style books usually have instructions on how to mark a manuscript page before submitting it to a printer.

Be certain that each quote in a speaker's paper has a footnote stating the source. An illustration being reprinted from a copyrighted source must have a source note and permission to use it in the book must have been secured from the copyright holder. Remind the Program Committee to advise speakers that they must submit letters of permission from the owners of copyrighted material used in their papers. They should also submit illustrations with each paper carefully keyed for position in the paper.

As you edit the paper, check each illustration as well. Mark off the portions of a photograph that you don't want to use. So that you don't crease a photograph while doing this, use a grease pencil to make crop marks in the white borders of the photograph or a felt-tip pen to write on the back of the photograph. For lengthy comments or instructions, attach a separate piece of paper to the white margin of a photograph.

Style Sheet. Whether you use an outside printer or an in-house desktop publishing department, keep a style sheet as you edit and submit it along with the manuscript. Note on the sheet how you have edited different things—words, abbreviations, subheads, tables, and so on—for style and consistency from paper to paper.

For example, state how you have treated numbers (*ten* or *10*), prefixes (*nontraditional* or *non-traditional*), and suffixes (*sand-like* or *sandlike*). Indicate how you have treated footnotes—paragraph indent or flush left, with raised numbers or numbers set on the line. State how you edited special terms for capitalization—*Republican party* or *Republican Party*. Also note anything else you edited for style and consistency, such as setting quotes of eight lines or more as indented blocks of copy (extracts).

As you edit, don't trust your memory in matters of style. Unless these points are written on a style sheet that you can refer to, it's unlikely that you'll remember from chapter to chapter how something is hyphenated, capitalized, spelled, or formatted.

Although a computer operator may use a spell-checker to correct errors, you should still proofread every page of set copy. Some text may have been omitted or paragraphs accidentally set out of order. Also, a spell-checker will not catch all errors, such as *the* when *then* is intended.

Page Design. Whether you're using an outside service or an in-house desktop publisher to produce the book, provide your own specifications to follow, or ask to see sample pages. Samples should include spacing (around headings and other elements), chapter titles and subheads, footnotes, and other parts of each chapter. If the appearance doesn't suit you, ask for changes and new sample pages.

Find out how you should mark the pages in regard to design. The operators may need to have you mark the various elements on each page so that they know what type size and layout to use for each one. You may use letters that you circle beside each element on the manuscript page, for example: CT = chapter title; A= first-level subhead; B= second-level subhead; C= third-level subhead; UT = unnumbered table; L = numbered list; ML = multicolumn list; FN = footnote; SN = source note (for photographs or drawings); and so on.

Disk Copy. You may be asked to submit a disk copy of each paper that the printer or desktop publishing department will use to convert the copy for each paper into a typeset form. Find out whether the speakers should prepare their disk copies in a certain way, such as by typing various codes in front of each element. If this is required, the initial instructions sent to speakers should include all such explanations.

Submission of Papers. Continue to work closely with the Program Committee in regard to the order of topics in the book (possibly to match the order on the program) and late papers. In the meantime, after you've approved the page design and type specifications and have a few papers edited, the computer operators or outside typesetter can begin keyboarding.

Although most printers prefer that you wait and submit all papers at once, there may not be enough time to handle the work in that way, especially if time is short and some papers are not expected until the last minute.

While production is in progress, monitor the schedule closely. Is everyone meeting the deadlines for each part of the job? With little time to spare, you may fall behind schedule if many papers are late.

Proofreading. Use a proofreading chart while marking the pages of proof. Most style books have such a chart with standard symbols used and recognized by professional writers, editors, typesetters, and printers. Whereas editing marks should be put directly on or between the lines of type on a double-spaced manuscript page, proofreading marks should be placed in the margins of a page proof.

Be certain that you see proofs of everything, including page proofs (usually showing text only, with an empty space where illustrations will go) and negative or press proofs (the final proof showing what each page will look like with illustrations in place). If you don't check the final proof, you may find that a photograph belonging on page 5 in the first chapter somehow got printed on page 67 in the third chapter. Whether your company or a printer is designing the cover, insist on seeing, first, a layout and, then, a proof.

Delivery. Monitor the concluding stages of production through binding. Check with the printer to ensure that the bound copies are being shipped to the conference site on schedule.

Deliver advance copies to the Program Committee and the Planning Committee, and advise the Registration and Facilities committees that copies are being delivered to the conference site. The Facilities Committee, in conjunction with the hotel, should arrange for storage until the conference opens, and the Registration Committee will likely be in charge of proceedings handouts or sales to registrants.

After the meeting, or upon completion of the printing job, arrange for the return of surplus copies to the designated office. Then review final bills and forward them to the designated person for payment. File your style sheet, the design specifications, and other material related to production in a meeting folder for use by future meeting arrangers. Finally, undertake a postmeeting evaluation of the minutes and proceedings arrangements and submit a concluding report to the Planning Committee.

MEETING CONDUCT: THE NEW ROBERT'S RULES OF ORDER

INTRODUCTION TO
THE RULES

In the Preface to the 1893 edition of *Robert's Rules of Order,* General H. M. Robert began by stating that "a work on parliamentary law has long been needed, based, in its general principles, upon the rules and practice of Congress, but adapted, in its details, to the use of ordinary societies." If he were writing this introduction he would probably begin by stating that "a work on parliamentary law is needed as much today as it was in 1893." Perhaps it is needed even more, since there are more people and more organized groups holding meetings than ever before.

The importance of the 1893 edition and the validity of its content here have never been contested, and *The New Robert's Rules of Order* is a testimony to its worth rather than an indictment of its diminished value. Although some changes have occurred in the rules of parliamentary procedure, the original rules, by and large, still apply.

However, a lot of other things have changed in the world since 1893. Perhaps most obvious are changes in the written and spoken language that we use. Some people, especially school-age readers and young adults in the working world, are distracted and confused by the writing style that was appropriate more than a hundred years ago. To some, then, the meaning of the text is lost in the prose. This points to a principal aim of *The New Robert's Rules of Order:* to present all of General Robert's rules and commentary in contemporary English.

The complete and official text of the 1893 edition included notes appended to the various sections, highlighting rule changes that had occurred since General Robert's first book of rules had been published in 1876. Whereas such revisions appear as separate "Notes" in the 1893 version, they're blended into the text in *The New Robert's Rules of Order* so the updated information is conveyed in a less obtrusive, easier to comprehend style. The changes, then, are no longer presented as notes to the main text but are treated as the updated text itself.

One thing has not been changed in *The New Robert's Rules of Order:* the organization of the contents. Although persuasive arguments could be developed for changing the organization of material, one important factor prevailed—the objective of this new version is to simplify and clarify the *original* text so that readers can follow and comprehend it more easily. Therefore, we didn't want to do anything that might cause confusion.

Changing the order of topics to which readers have become accustomed over the years could well invite confusion. If you were at a meeting and a question arose, you might want to discuss with others a certain point in the book of rules. If the appropriate section were numbered 15 in your book and 21 in someone else's edition, this confusion would cause unnecessary delay. In the interest of consistency, therefore, this version retains the same order of topics, the same chapter and article titles, and the same section numbers as the 1893 edition. Only the text within each section has been rewritten in a modern, more readable style.

Like the 1893 edition, this edition also divides the text information on parliamentary procedure into three parts: I. Rules of Order; II. Organization and Conduct of Business; and III. Miscellaneous. For a complete list of topics, refer to the table of contents in the front of the book and, especially, to the general index at the end of the book. For information about meeting matters other than parliamentary procedure, review the chapters at the beginning of the book concerning meeting arrangements.

Parliamentary Law

Originally, *parliamentary law* referred to the customs and rules of conducting business in the English Parliament. Now, in the United States, it also refers to the customs and rules of conducting business in U.S. legislative assembles. As long as these customs and rules don't conflict with other rules or precedents that already exist, they're considered *the* authority for the conduct of business in assembled groups.

U.S. organizations, however, have different needs from those of the English parliament, and the rules have been changed from time to time to fit those needs. Individual organizations in the United States have also modified the rules to fit their own particular needs. On the national level, the House of Representatives, for instance, doesn't use the same rules that the Senate uses. The *exact* method of conducting business in any organization, therefore, depends on that organization's specific needs, legal requirements, and established rules and precedents.

Parliamentary law in the United States has thus superseded English parliamentary law in ordinary groups that assemble to conduct business. Groups of all types and sizes, from those of small local clubs to large national organizations, have needed some system of conducting business and a set of rules to govern their proceedings. The unique system of parliamentary law developed in the United States has become the "common law" of these ordinary organizations.

The two houses of the U.S. Congress follow different rules in some respects. For ordinary groups, the *final* authority for all great parliamentary questions (such as what motions can be made and what is the proper order of precedence or which ones can be debated and what is their effect) is the practice of the U.S. House of Representatives—not the Senate, the English Parliament, or any other body.

The Senate rules, for example, don't allow one to make a motion calling for the Previous Question [asking that debate stop and a matter be brought to a vote] (Section 20), and they make a motion to Postpone [a matter] Indefinitely (Section 24) take precedence over every other subsidiary motion (see Section 7) except to Lay [a matter] on the Table (Section 19). But the House recognizes the Previous Question as a legitimate motion and assigns the motion to Postpone Indefinitely to the very lowest rank.

In other matters, though, ordinary groups wouldn't necessarily follow the House rules. The chair in the House, for example, can order that the galleries be cleared or that a bill must be read three times before its passage. Such matters are inappropriate for other organizations. Yet, in conducting business, when an organization can't decide a case clearly or easily, it should imitate the rules of the legislative bodies.

Plan of the Work

The rules of order in this book are generally suitable for ordinary (nonlegislative) groups and should be sufficient for most organizations until they need to adopt other rules to meet some special requirement. The rules are based on the practice of Congress except when the practice is not appropriate for ordinary groups. But even then the rules in Congress are given for comparison. In important matters, the rules given here are used by the House of Representatives.

One of the exceptions to House rules recommended for ordinary groups concerns the vote required to pass a measure. The House uses a bare majority to take final action on a question without allowing any discussion. But ordinary groups need to consider the rights of minorities. They should therefore require a two-thirds vote to sustain an objection to introducing a motion, to adopt a motion calling for the Previous Question (Section 20), or to adopt an order closing or limiting debate (see Section 39).

In this book a majority is needed to order a vote by "yeas and nays" (see Section 38), and this rule is best for most organizations. Congress, on the other hand, needs only a one-fifth vote, and in some organizations a single member can require that a vote be taken by "yeas and nays."

An organization may use the rules given here when they're appropriate and consistent with the group's own rules of order and bylaws (see Section 49 for the form of a rule that an organization can adopt for this purpose). An organization's own rules should cover all of those cases when it's necessary to depart from the rules in this book and, especially, should provide for a quorum (see Section 43) and an order of business (see Section 44).

The text of this book is divided into three distinct parts, followed by a quick-reference section including a table of rules for easy reference in the midst of the business of a meeting.

Part I

The first part (pages 106–196) has a set of rules arranged systematically (as shown in the table of contents) in forty-five sections. Each section is complete in itself so that you can examine selected subjects without being misled. However, each section also has cross-references to other sections that are related or are important to the subject under consideration.

The motions are arranged by order of rank under their traditional classes. (Note, however, that motions are listed *alphabetically* in the index at the back of the book and in the table of motions at the end of the book.) The following information is given in regard to each motion:

- A list of other motions over which a particular motion takes precedence (i.e., other motions that may be pending while it is nevertheless proper to make and consider a particular motion)

- Other motions to which a particular motion yields (i.e., other motions that may be made and considered while a particular motion is pending)

- Whether the motion is debatable (all motions are debatable unless stated otherwise)

- Whether a motion can be amended

- Which motions cannot have a subsidiary motion applied to them (see Section 11, Adjourn, for an example: the motion to Adjourn can't be laid on the table, postponed, committed, or amended)

- The effect of a motion, if adopted, when it might be misunderstood

- The form of stating a motion when it's unusual and any other information necessary to understand it

Part II

The second part (pages 197–244) is a parliamentary primer. It gives simple illustrations of the methods of organizing and conducting different kinds of meetings and the sample wording to follow when making and putting motions to a vote. It also outlines the duties of officers, the forms of minutes, and the forms of treasurer and committee reports. Finally, it classifies the motions in eight categories according to their objective, examines each class and compares the motions in it, and explains when each motion should be used.

Part III

The third part (pages 245–252) discusses miscellaneous matters that are important to assemblies, including the commonly misunderstood subject of the legal rights of deliberative assemblies or ecclesiastical tribunals.

Quick-Reference Guide to Motions

After the third part and just before the main index at the back of the book (pages 258–259) is a table of rules about motions for quick reference during a meeting. This is followed by a list showing the precedence of motions and a lit of forms (wording) for putting certain motions to a vote.

Definitions and Common Errors

To avoid misunderstanding when you read the following text, note the special meanings of the following terms:

Accepting a Report. Adopting (not receiving) a report (see Section 30 for common error in acting on reports).

Assembly. An organized body meeting to conduct business. When making a motion, substitute the term that applies to your group: *club, society, board, convention,* and so on.

Congress. Generally, in reference to rules, the U.S. House of Representatives (not the Senate).

Meeting and Session. The word *meeting* refers to an assembly of members gathered for any length of time without adjournment. A *session* includes all of the adjourned (continued) meetings (see Section 42).

Previous Question. A motion calling for an end to debate and requiring that a vote be taken on the pending matter (see Section 20).

Shall the Question Be Discussed. The traditional form of stating the motion about considering a subject; a negative vote dismisses the matter for that session (see Section 15).

Substitute. This motion is one form of an amendment. The five forms are given in note 3 to the table of rules in the Quick-Reference Guide (see also Section 23).

PART I.
RULES OF ORDER

Since this part thoroughly covers the rules of order, some of you will be primarily interested in this material, especially if you already have a basic knowledge of parliamentary law. But if the rules seem difficult to understand at first reading, skip over to Part II, which is a parliamentary primer, and read it first; then return to Part I.

Article I. Introduction of Business

Section 1. Introducing Business

To bring business before an assembled group, you can make a motion or present a communication. For ordinary, routine matters, however, groups that are gathered for a meeting (sometimes referred to as an *assembly* in this book) may dispense with the formality of a motion. The chair can then simply announce that the matter is adopted if there is no objection. But if a member of the assembly objects, the group must act by way of a regular motion.

Section 2. Obtaining the Floor

Before you can make a motion or address the assembly on any matter, you have to obtain the right to speak, or "obtain the floor." This means that you have to stand up (in a formal setting) and address the presiding officer (often referred to as the "chair" or "president") by his or her title, for example:

Madam President

Mr. Chairman

The chair will then recognize you by announcing your name or (if not known) by nodding in your direction:

The chair recognizes Ms. Davis.

But if the chair rises to speak before you obtain the floor, you must take your seat for the time being (see Section 36).

If you're conducting the meeting, it's up to you to recognize the member trying to get your attention. But what if two or more persons stand up at the same time? Who is entitled to speak to the assembly? (If there are any doubts about who should have the floor, you can always allow the assembly to decide by vote, with the person receiving the largest vote obtaining the floor.) Robert's rules of order recommend that you be guided by these principles in making a decision:

- Recognize the person who previously made a motion being discussed or the one who presented a committee report currently under discussion (unless he or she already has had the floor during the discussion), even though another individual may have stood up and addressed the chair first.

- No one who has had the floor previously may have it again while the same matter is before the assembly if someone else who hasn't yet spoken asks to be recognized. (See Section 26 for details on what to do if you want to change a motion before an assembly.)

- Make an effort to allow both sides of a matter to be presented; if someone has spoken on one side of a measure, try to recognize next someone who will address the other side of the issue.

- Don't recognize someone who stood up and remained standing while another person was speaking if still another individual rises after the speaker finishes and yields the floor.

If others object to your decision in recognizing someone, any two members can appeal your decision. But the House of Representatives doesn't allow such an appeal. In other large assemblies, too, such an appeal is not desirable, since the chair needs to have more power to handle a large group and maintain order.

Once the floor is assigned to someone, no one—neither the chair nor another member of the assembly—should interrupt that person by calling for a vote on a motion, by making a motion to Adjourn (Section 11), or by doing anything else. (But see the exceptions listed below.) A chair, then, should try to protect the rights of a speaker who has the floor.

> *Ms. Jackson:* Therefore, we need to consider other alternatives.

> *Mr. Barnes:* Mr. Chairman, I move that we appoint a committee to research the subject.

> *Chair:* Sir, the motion is out of order. Ms. Jackson has the floor.

There are five exceptions to the rule about not interrupting a member who has been given the floor; it may, therefore, be necessary to interrupt someone for these reasons:

1. To enter in the minutes a motion to Reconsider (Section 27)

2. To allow a Question of Order (Section 14)

3. To recognize an Objection to the Consideration of a Question (Section 15)

4. To call for the Orders of the Day (Section 13)

5. To admit a Question of Privilege that requires immediate action (see Section 12)

A person who interrupts for a legitimate reason should state his or her purpose for doing so:

Mr. Chairman, I rise to a point of order [*want to point out a breach of parliamentary rules***].**

Assume that a member obtains the floor and makes a motion that is in order (allowed) and is debatable. If that motion isn't seconded immediately, you, as chair, should ask:

Does anyone want to second the motion to ___?

A member can second it, without rising, by simply stating:

I second the motion [*or* **I second the motion to ___].**

Until members have had time to second a motion, you shouldn't allow any other motion to be made. Even then, after the first motion is seconded, no one should make a new motion until the person who made the first one decides to yield the floor; in fact, if necessary or appropriate, you might ask:

Will Mr. Billingsley yield the floor now?

Motions to Adjourn (Section 11) and to Lay [a matter] on the Table (Section 19) are often made incorrectly (a) by persons who don't have the floor, (b) after someone has just made another motion, and (c) while the person making the other motion is still entitled to the floor. A chair shouldn't recognize such new motions. (But see Article III on motions and their order of precedence.)

A person who submits a committee report or offers a resolution doesn't lose the floor by asking the secretary to read it. The secretary doesn't thereby gain the floor—and the chair can't accept a motion made by the secretary—unless the person who submits the report or resolution yields the floor.

Usually, after the secretary finishes reading the material, the person submitting it resumes the floor and makes a motion that it be adopted. The chair should then recognize the person as having the floor and repeat the motion ("state the question"). However, a member who wants to make a motion that is "in order" (proper) when someone else has the floor could interrupt that person at any time. (See the table of rules and list of precedence of motions in the Quick-Reference Guide.)

Section 3. What Precedes Debate on a Question

Before any subject is open to debate (see Section 34), three things are necessary:

1. A motion must be made by a member who has the floor (see Section 46 for examples of various forms of making motions):

   I move that we adopt the Maxwell proposal.

2. The motion must be seconded:

   I second the motion.

   Exceptions: A call for Orders of the Day (Section 13), a question of order but not an Appeal (Section 14), and an Objection to the Consideration of a Question (Section 15) do not have to be seconded. (In Congress, motions don't have to be seconded; even in ordinary assemblies, routine motions are not always made, and some are never seconded; the presiding officer merely announces that, if no one objects, the matter will be adopted or considered the action of the assembly.)

3. The motion must be stated by the presiding officer (see Section 65 for forms of stating questions):

   The motion to adopt the Maxwell proposal has been seconded. It's now open to debate.

Before the chair states the motion, though, the person making it can modify or withdraw it. *After* the chair states it, the person must get the consent of the assembly to modify or withdraw it (see Sections 5 and 17). When a person withdraws or modifies a motion, the member who seconded it can also withdraw his or her second. The series of remarks might resemble this:

> *Ms. Adams:* I move that we adopt the Maxwell proposal.

> *Mr. Brubaker:* I second the motion.

> *Mr. Adams:* Before the chair reads the motion, I'd like to modify it to read: "I move we adopt the Maxwell proposal as amended on January 9, 19XX."

> *Mr. Brubaker:* I then withdraw my second.

> *Chair:* Does anyone want to second Ms. Adam's modified statement?

> *Mr. Donatelli:* I second the modified motion.

> *Chair:* The motion to adopt the Maxwell proposal as amended on January 9, 19XX, has been seconded. It's now open to debate.

Section 4. What Motions Must Be in Writing and How They Should Be Divided

All principal motions (see Section 6), amendments, and instructions to committees should be in writing—if required by the presiding officer. Sometimes a motion is complicated and could be simplified by dividing it into several less complex motions. But unless a special rule allows a member to ask for this to be done, he or she can't insist on it. Instead, anyone who wants this done should make a motion to that effect and indicate in the motion how the particular matter can be divided. But someone else can then make another motion, such as an amendment, to divide it differently.

Division of a Question. The division of a question, or motion, is really an amendment and subject to the same rules (see Section 23). Therefore, instead of moving to divide a motion, you could make a motion for some other form of amendment.

For a motion to be divided, each separate motion that results must be something the assembly can act on even if the other resulting motions aren't adopted. A motion to Commit (Section 22) with instructions, therefore, can't be divided because if the motion to Commit should fail, the motion to instruct the committee wouldn't make sense (there wouldn't be any committee to instruct).

According to Rule 46 of the House, a motion must be divided upon the demand of one member if it "comprehends propositions in substance so distinct that one being taken away a substantive proposition shall remain for the decision of the House." This doesn't mean that a motion can be divided just to enable to vote on separate items or names. Rule 121, however, states that one-fifth of the members can demand a vote on separate or collective items, as specified in the call, in the case of a bill making appropriations for internal improvements. But this right to divide a motion into items extends only to the case specified. Common parliamentary law doesn't allow for division unless the assembly orders it, and in ordinary assemblies, this rule is more appropriate than that of the House.

A motion to strike out certain words and insert others can't be divided because, usually, the two steps belong together; that is, both must occur to make sense.

Section 5. Modifications of a Motion by Mover

After a chair has stated a motion, it's open to debate by members of the assembly. The person making the motion can no longer withdraw or modify it, if anyone objects, without getting the approval of the assembly to withdraw it (see Section 17) or by making a motion for an amendment (see Section 3).

According to Rule 40 of the House: "After a motion is stated by the Speaker, or read by the Clerk, it shall be deemed to be in the possession of the House, but may be withdrawn at any time before a decision or amendment." The practice in the House has been *not* to allow a motion to be withdrawn after the Previous Question (Section 20) has been seconded. The rules of order in this book conform to the old parliamentary principle, which is more suitable for ordinary assemblies. Some groups, though, may prefer to follow the practice of the House.

Article II. General Classification of Motions

Section 6. Principal, or Main, Motions

A *principal,* or *main, motion,* also known as a principal, or main, question, is a motion on any particular subject brought before an assembly for consideration. However, you can't make a principal motion when another motion is before the assembly. Since a principal motion does *not* have precedence over any other motion, it yields to all secondary motions, incidental motions, and privileged motions (see Sections 7, 8, and 9).

A motion is out of order if it conflicts with the organization's charter, articles of incorporation, or constitution; bylaws; standing orders; or resolutions, as well as any resolution adopted during the sessions (see Section 42). Such a motion might be adopted in error, but it would be null and void. To introduce such a motion, the assembly would have to rescind any conflicting rule or resolution or amend the charter, articles of incorporation, constitution, or bylaws. (Note that the motion to Reconsider [Section 27] isn't a principal motion; it's a motion that brings a matter before the assembly *again*.)

Section 7. Subsidiary, or Secondary, Motions

A *subsidiary,* or *secondary, motion* is a motion applied to another motion as a means of disposing of the other motion (in other words, the two motions are made together at the same time).

> *Example:* **A motion to have an Appeal (Section 14) Lay on the Table (Section 19) is a secondary motion because it enables the assembly to dispose of the Appeal. The Appeal, meanwhile, is an incidental question that arises because some members object to a decision of the chair.**

A subsidiary motion has precedence over a principal motion and has to be decided before the assembly can act on the principal motion. But a subsidiary motion yields to privileged and incidental motions (see Sections 8 and 9). The six subsidiary motions are listed here in order of precedence:

1. To Lay [a matter] on the Table (Section 19)

2. To order the Previous Question (Section 20)

3. To Postpone [something] to a Certain Day (Section 21)

4. To Commit, or Refer, something (Section 22)

5. To Amend something (Section 23)

6. To Postpone [something] Indefinitely (Section 24)

You can make any of these subsidiary motions except the one to Amend when another lower-order motion is pending. But you can't make a subsidary motion if one of a higher order is pending. Subsidiary motions can't be "applied" to one another except in the following cases:

- A call for the Previous Question can be applied to the motion to Postpone without affecting the principal motion and can, if specified, be applied to a pending amendment (see Section 20).

- The motions to Postpone to a Certain Day, to Commit, and to Amend can be amended.

- A motion to Amend a certain part of the minutes can be tabled (see Section 19) without carrying all of the minutes with it.

Section 8. Incidental Motions

Incidental motions arise out of or are prompted by other motions and, therefore, take precedence over and must be decided before the other motions. But they yield to privileged motions (see Section 9) and can't be amended. All incidental motions except an Appeal are undebatable; an Appeal may or may not be debated (see Section 14). The five incidental motions are listed here in order of precedence:

1. To Appeal, or raise Questions of Order (Section 14)

2. To Object to the Consideration of a Question (Section 15)

3. To request the Reading of Papers (Section 16)

4. To Withdraw a Motion (Section 17)

5. To Suspend the Rules (Section 18)

Section 9. Privileged Motions

Privileged motions are not related to a pending motion but, because of their importance, take precedence over all other motions. They can't be debated (see Section 35) unless they pertain to the rights of the assembly or its members; therefore, they can't be used to interrupt business. The four privileged motions are listed here in order of precedence:

1. To Fix the Time to Which to Adjourn (Section 10)

2. To Adjourn (Section 11)

3. To raise Questions of Privilege (Section 12)

4. To call for the Orders of the Day (Section 13)

Article III. Motions and Their Order of Precedence

The ordinary motions are arranged in order of precedence in the Precedence of Motions list provided in the Quick-Reference Guidance to Motions. The privileged motions (see Sections 10–13) and the subsidiary motions (see Sections 19–24) are discussed here in order of precedence.

Privileged Motions

Section 10. To Fix the Time to Which to Adjourn

The motion to Fix the Time to Which to Adjourn (to set the time of a continued meeting) takes precedence over all other motions. In fact, this motion is in order even after the assembly has voted to adjourn provided the chair hasn't yet announced the result of the vote on adjournment.

If you make a motion to Fix the Time to Which to Adjourn when another motion is before the assembly, it's not debatable (see Section 35). It can be amended, though, by altering the time. If you make this motion when no other motion is before the assembly, it's treated the same as any other principal motion (see Section 6) and in that case *is* debatable.

In ordinary groups it's best to follow common parliamentary law and introduce this motion as a principal motion rather than a privileged motion. Then it can be debated or suppressed (see Sections 58 and 59) like other motions. (In Congress, however, this motion can't be debated under any circumstances, and there it has entirely superseded the unprivileged and inferior motion to Adjourn to a particular time.)

A common form for stating the motion to Fix the Time to Which to Adjourn is as follows:

I move that when this assembly adjourns, it adjourn to meet at _____ time.

Section 11. To Adjourn

The motion to Adjourn, when it's not qualified, takes precedence over all others except the motion to Fix the Time to Which to Adjourn (Section 10). The motion to Adjourn can't be debated or amended, and it can't have a subsidiary motion (see Section 7) applied to it. Also a vote on adjournment can't be reconsidered. When a motion to Adjourn is qualified in some way, it loses its status as a privileged motion and becomes simply another principal motion (see Section 6).

You can repeat the motion to Adjourn if other business has intervened or if debate has progressed (see Section 26). But you can't make a motion to Adjourn if someone else has the floor. Also, you can't make this motion after another motion has been stated and is being put to a vote. But you can make the motion after the vote has been taken and before it has been announced. If that happens, the chair should announce the vote after business has resumed.

Sometimes, with elections and other time-consuming matters, it's best for a group to take a short recess (or transact other business) until the tellers have counted the ballots and are ready to report. (A *recess* is an adjournment of a group for a limited time during a session.) For example, to recess you might move:

That when we adjourn, we adjourn to meet at the call of the chair.

To end the recess, the chair would then call the meeting to order as soon as the ballots are counted. Or you could move to take a recess of fifteen (or other) minutes. This would be in order unless there is a pending motion to

Adjourn or another motion has been made and the assembly is voting on it.

An assembly may vote down a motion to Adjourn if the participants want to hear another speech or take another vote. But since that's true, it's necessary to be able to renew the motion afterward.

The chair should take steps to ensure that this privilege isn't abused. If you were conducting a meeting, for example, and the group had just voted down a motion to Adjourn, you should refuse to consider another motion to Adjourn if nothing else had yet occurred. The group in this case presumably would still not want to adjourn until other business was transacted. Also, as chair, you shouldn't consider any appeal or points of order after someone has moved to Adjourn unless the assembly has voted down the motion.

Some business is referred to committees. When a committee is through with any business referred to it and is ready to report, someone should make a motion to Rise. This motion in a committee has the same privileges as a motion to Adjourn in the full assembly.

An adjournment affects unfinished business as follows:

- When some unfinished business occurs at the end of a meeting but not at the close of a session, it should be the first order of business, after the reading of the minutes, at the next meeting in that session. It then would be treated as though there had been no adjournment. (An *adjourned meeting* is legally the continuation of a meeting that had previously adjourned to meet later.) The assembly, however, may adopt rules that modify this general rule.

- When some unfinished business occurs at the end of a session and the assembly has more than one regular session each year, the unfinished business is taken up at the next session, before the introduction of "new business," and it's still treated as though there had been no adjournment (see Section 44 for its place in the order of business). But in a body elected for a specific term (one year, for example), unfinished business is simply dropped at the end of the term.

- When an adjournment closes a session in an assembly that meets only once a year, or when the assembly is an elective body and the session ends the term of some of the members, the unfinished business also ends at the close of the session. But it can be introduced at the next session as if it had never been before the assembly.

According to Rule 136 of the House, after six days from the beginning of a second or subsequent session of any Congress, all bills, resolutions, and reports that originated in the House and are undecided at the close of the next preceding session must be resumed and acted on as though there had been no adjournment. But unfinished business doesn't go from one Congress to another. Any ordinary group that meets only once a year would likely have a different membership each year (just as each new congressional composition may be different). In that case, it would be unwise for it to carry unfinished business to a future year.

Section 12. Questions of Privilege

Questions of Privilege are motions pertaining to the rights and privileges of the assembly or any of its members. They take precedence over all other motions except the motions to Fix the Time to Which to Adjourn (Section 10) and to Adjourn (Section 11).

Questions of Privilege aren't the same thing as privileged questions. (Privileged questions include Questions of Privilege; see Section 9.) Examples of Questions of Privilege are disorder in the gallery, one member opening a window and causing a draft that endangers the health of others, or charges against the official character of a member. For instance:

> *Mr. Wright (speaker):* I therefore recommend that . . .
>
> *Member (interrupting):* **Madam President, I move that the window just opened along the left aisle be closed. The cold wind is bothering those of us in its path.**
>
> *President:* **Will the member seated by the window please close it? You may continue, Mr. Wright.**

If a Question of Privilege requires immediate action, it can interrupt a member's speech. But the chair must decide if a question is really a Question of Privilege. Even if the chair rules that it is, any two members can appeal that decision.

Suppose that an assembly doesn't want to take final action on a Question of Privilege when it's raised. The question, then, might be referred to a committee (see Section 22). Or it might be tabled (see Section 19). Or it might have another subsidiary motion (see Section 7) applied to it. In that case, the subsidiary motion would be decided (disposed of) without affecting the motion that was interrupted by the Question of Privilege. As soon as the Question of Privilege is disposed of, the assembly may return to considering the original matter that was interrupted.

Section 13. Orders of the Day

Orders of the Day refers to the scheduling of subjects to be considered in a meeting. A call for the Orders of the Day (to stick to the scheduled order of business) takes precedence over every other motion except the motions to Reconsider (Section 27), to Fix the Time to Which to Adjourn (Section 10), and to Adjourn (Section 11) and except for Questions of Privilege (Section 12).

A call for the Orders of the Day can't be debated and can't be amended. Moreover, it doesn't have to be seconded, and it's in order even when another person has the floor:

Ms. Jacobs (speaker): Unless we act . . .

Mr. Hill (interrupting): Mr. Chairman, I move that we take up business as scheduled on the agenda.

Chair: The chair recognizes Mr. Hill.

Mr. Hill: Mr. Chairman, we were supposed to be considering the Newtown zoning plan at this time.

Chair: Thank you, Mr. Hill. Ms. Jacobs will now yield the floor, and we'll move on to the zoning plan.

Rule 54 of the House provides that at the close of the morning hour devoted to committee reports and resolutions, a motion is in order to move on to "the business on the Speaker's [of the House] table and to the orders of the day." It then specifies the order in which the business will be considered and states that "the messages, communications, and bills on his table having been disposed of, the Speaker shall then proceed to call the orders of the day." Although in Congress it is not in order to interrupt a member to call for the Orders of the Day, at the close of the morning hour a member may, even though someone else has the floor, move to proceed to "the business on the Speaker's table and to the orders of the day." To apply the House principle to ordinary groups, it's necessary to allow a motion calling for the Orders of the Day to interrupt a member who has the floor after the time has arrived for their consideration.

When one or more subjects have been assigned to a particular day or hour, they become the Orders of the Day for that time. They can't be considered before then except by a two-thirds vote (see Section 39).

When the specific time arrives, if the orders are called

up, they take precedence over all motions except the ones to Fix the Time to Which to Adjourn (Section 10), to Adjourn (Section 11), and to Reconsider (Section 27), as well as Questions of Privilege (Section 12).

Instead of considering the subjects at that time, however, the assembly may appoint another time for their consideration. If a matter isn't taken up at the new time, then the order is dropped.

Orders of the Day involve two classes: General Orders and Special Orders. The Special Orders always take precedence over the General Orders.

General Orders. These orders can be made by a majority by postponing questions to certain times or by adopting a program or order of business for the day or session. The General Orders, however, must not interfere with any established rules of an assembly.

Special Orders. A Special Order suspends all of the rules of an assembly that interfere with its consideration at the time specified. It therefore requires a two-thirds vote to make any matter a Special Order. (If a group had adopted the order of business as described in Section 44, when the specified time arrived, anyone could call for Special Orders even though a committee might be reporting at the time. But the Orders for the Day in general could not be called for until all of the committee's reports had been acted on.)

A call for Special Orders is in order whenever a motion to Suspend the Rules (Section 18) is in order. Once a Special Order is made for a particular time, it's not in order to make another Special Order that would precede or interfere with the first one. Yet a Special Order may interfere with General Orders.

When the Orders of the Day are taken up, the Special Orders must be considered first and then the General Orders. Within each class—Special or General Orders—the individual questions must be taken up in their exact order. If two or more matters are assigned to the same day or hour, the one that was assigned first takes precedence over the others. (A motion to take up a particular part of the Orders of the Day, or a certain matter, is not a privileged motion.)

Any subject, when taken up, can be assigned to another time instead of being considered then. In fact, a majority can postpone even a Special Order.

Common forms of this question as stated by the chair when the proper time arrives—or in response to the call of a member—would be similar to the examples shown here:

Are we ready to take up the Orders of the Day?

Shall the Orders of the Day be taken up?

Will the assembly now proceed to the Orders of the Day?

An *affirmative* vote on a call for the Orders of the Day effectively removes any other motion being considered by the assembly the same as if it had been interrupted by an adjournment (see Section 11). A *negative* vote on the call effectively stops the scheduled business from interfering with a consideration of another motion before the assembly.

When one subject is being considered and the time assigned to another subject arrives, the chair should announce that it's time to move on to the next assigned subject, putting the previous motion to an immediate vote. But if a member objects to moving on to the next subject, the chair should ask:

Will the assembly now proceed to consider [*subject*] that was assigned to this hour?

Since it takes a formal vote (except by unanimous consent) to proceed to the Orders of the Day, it also takes a formal vote afterward to move on to the next assigned topic if anyone objects to closing discussion on the previous topic.

Incidental Motions

Section 14. To Appeal (Questions of Order)

A Question of Order (point of order) is a motion or objection by someone concerning the violation of a rule. It

takes precedence over the motion that prompted it, and it
has to be decided by the presiding officer without a debate.

However, a motion can't be ruled out of order after
it already has been entertained and debated without objection. A formal Appeal can be made only at the time
of the decision of the chair. At that time, if a member
objects to the chair's decision, he or she might state:

I appeal from the decision of the chair.

If the Appeal is seconded, the chair should immediately
explain the basis for the decision and state the motion:

Shall the decision of the chair be sustained?

**Shall the decision of the chair stand as the judg-
ment of the assembly [or "board, society," and
so on]?**

If there's a tie vote, the decision of the chair stands.
(See Section 65 for details on the method of stating the
motion on an Appeal.)

This Appeal yields to privileged questions (see Section
9). It can't be amended. Also, it can't be debated when
it relates simply to impropriety (see Section 36), to transgressions of the rules of speaking, or to the priority of
business or if it's made while the Previous Question
(Section 20) is pending.

When a matter is debatable, a member may speak
only once. The presiding officer, however, may (without
leaving the chair) state the reasons for his or her decision on the Appeal. Also, if the Appeal is debatable,
the motion to Lay [a matter] on the Table (Section 19)
and the Previous Question (Section 20) can be applied
to it. When adopted, these motions will affect nothing
but the Appeal (not the matter being appealed).

The vote on an Appeal may be reconsidered (see Section 27). But an Appeal is not in order when another
Appeal is pending. (In Congress the usual course in case
of an Appeal is to table it, since this effectively kills it
and sustains the decision of the chair.)

The presiding officer must enforce the rules and orders of the assembly without debate or delay. A member may, in fact, insist on it, saying something such as this:

Point of order.

Madam Chairman, I rise to a point of order.

The person who was speaking when the member interrupted would then sit down, and the chair would ask the member that interrupted to state his or her point of order. The member might, for instance, state that the speaker was suggesting action that would violate the group's bylaws.

The chair has to make a decision on a point of order. For example, he or she might overrule the objection and ask the speaker to continue or might find the objection to be in order and instruct the speaker to conform to the rules. But if the decision is that the speaker's remarks are improper and if someone objects to having the speaker continue, the assembly must vote on the matter.

I call the speaker to order.

The chair would then decide if the speaker's language is in or out of order. In deciding such Questions of Order, a chair might ask the advice of members. In such cases, to avoid the appearance of debate, members should remain seated when giving advice. Another alternative is for the chair to submit a motion to the assembly for a vote.

Section 15. Objection to Consideration of a Question

In a meeting, you can object to having the assembly consider any principal, or main, motion (see Section 6) but only when the motion is first introduced, before it has been debated. Such an objection is similar to a Question of Order (Section 14) in that you can make it while someone else has the floor and it doesn't require a second. Just as the chair can call a member to order, he or she can make a decision about whether an objection to considering a motion is in order.

An Objection to Consideration of a Question can't be debated (see Section 35) or amended (see Section 23). It also can't have any subsidiary motion (see Section 7) applied to it.

When someone makes a motion and another member objects to considering it, the chair must immediately put the motion to a vote, stating it in a form such as one of the following:

Will the assembly consider it?

Shall the motion be considered?

If two-thirds of the members vote no (see Section 39), the subject is dropped for that session (see Section 42). If two-thirds vote yes, the discussion continues as though the motion had never come up.

The purpose of making a motion objecting to the consideration of another motion is not to cut off debate on the objectionable question; other motions are available for that (see Section 37). The objective is to give the assembly a chance to avoid motions that the members might view as irrelevant, unprofitable, or contentious.

According to Rule 41 of the House, the introduction of motions that the members might want to avoid can be prevented temporarily by a majority vote: "Where any motion or proposition is made, the question 'Will the House now consider it?' shall not be put unless it is demanded by some member or is deemed necessary by the Speaker." (See Section 39.) The English use the Previous Question (Section 20) for a similar purpose.

The question of consideration is seldom raised in Congress. But in other organizations with short sessions and little time for a lot of motions, it's essential that two-thirds of the members be able to throw out subjects they don't want to consider.

Section 16. Reading Papers

Members may ask to have papers that are brought before the assembly read once before voting on them. (See Section 8 for the order of precedence of Reading Papers.) When a member asks to have a paper read, clearly for information and not as a delaying tactic, the chair should call for it to be read if no one objects. Except for this, members don't have the right to have just any material read without permission from the assembly. The motion or request to grant such permission can't be debated or amended.

Section 17. Withdrawal of a Motion

When a motion is before an assembly and the person who made the motion wants to withdraw or modify it or substitute another motion, the chair should grant permission if no one objects. (See Section 8 for the order of precedence for the Withdrawal of a Motion.) But if someone objects, the chair will have to put the question on granting the request to a vote, or someone can make a motion to grant it. A motion to withdraw another motion can't be debated or amended. When a motion is withdrawn, the effect is the same as if it had never been made.

According to Rule 40 of the House, in Congress a motion may be withdrawn by the mover before a decision or amendment is made. But in ordinary groups, nothing would be gained by deviating from the old common law stated in Section 17. (See also Section 5.)

Section 18. Suspension of the Rules

The motion to Suspend the Rules can't be debated; moreover, it can't be amended, and a subsidiary motion (see Section 7) can't be applied to it. Also, a vote on it may not be reconsidered (see Section 27), nor can a motion to

Suspend a Rule for the same purpose be renewed (see Section 26) at the same meeting. However, the motion may be made again after an adjournment even when the next meeting is held on the same day. (In Congress, the motion can't be renewed the same day.) See Section 8 for the order of precedence of this motion.

The motion to Suspend the Rules applies only to an organization's rules of order or standing rules (see Section 49) since its charter, articles of incorporation, or constitution and its bylaws can't be suspended even by unanimous consent, unless they provide for their own suspension. But they should never be suspended except in the case of a bylaw relating to the transaction of business, and then the reason for the suspension should be specified.

The rules of an assembly, therefore, must not be suspended except for a definite purpose, and then a two-thirds vote is required. Also, no rule should be suspended, except by unanimous consent, that gives any right to a minority as small as one-third. It would be pointless, for example, to have a rule allowing one-fifth of the members present to order the "yeas and nays" (see Section 38 and 39) if two-thirds could simply suspend that rule.

A common form of this motion is as follows:

> I move to suspend the rules that interfere with _____.

Subsidiary Motions

Section 19. To Lay on the Table

The motion to Lay on the Table a particular subject (set it aside temporarily) takes precedence over all other subsidiary questions (see Section 7). But it yields to any incidental motion (see Section 8) or privileged motion (see Section 9). This motion is not debatable and can't be amended or have any other subsidiary motion applied to it. Also, an affirmative vote on it can't be reconsidered (see Section 27); it removes the subject from consideration until the assembly votes to take it from the table.

If a member incorrectly makes a motion to table some

matter for a specified time, the chair shouldn't rule it out of order but should recognize and restate it as a motion to Postpone [the matter] to a Certain Time (Section 21). The motion to Lay [a subject] on the Table can't be limited in any way. Some of the common forms of this motion are shown in these examples:

> **I move to lay the question of _____ on the table.**
>
> **I move that the matter of _____ be laid on the table.**

When someone wants to take up the matter again, one of the forms here should be followed:

> **I move to take the matter of _____ from the table.**
>
> **I move to take from the table the motion to _____.**

In organizations with sessions of a day or less, occurring as often as monthly, it should be permissible to take up any matter that was tabled at the previous session (see Section 42). In the case of a resolution, however, it would be better to offer it again as a new resolution.

The motion to Lay [a subject] on the Table has no privilege, is undebatable, and can't have any other subsidiary motion applied to it. The object of it is to temporarily set aside a subject so that it can be taken up at any time in the same or a future meeting. You couldn't accomplish this by a motion to Postpone [the matter] Indefinitely (Section 24) or definitely.

The motion also is used frequently to suppress a question (see Section 59) for a particular session. It can do this as long as there will never be a majority vote to take it from the table during that session (see Section 42).

The effect of the motion to Lay [a subject] on the Table is to set aside for that entire session (see Section 42) everything that pertains to the subject. For example, if an amendment is tabled, the subject to be amended goes there with it. The following cases, though, are exceptions:

- An Appeal (Section 14) that is tabled has the effect of sustaining, at least for the time being, the decision of the chair; it doesn't carry the original subject to the table with it.

- When a motion to Reconsider a Question (Section 27) is tabled, the original question is left where it was before moving to Reconsider; only the motion to Reconsider is set aside.

- When an amendment to the minutes is tabled, it doesn't carry the entire minutes with it.

A Question of Privilege (Section 12) doesn't pertain to the subject it may happen to interrupt; consequently, if it were set aside, the motion to Lay on the Table wouldn't carry with it the question that was interrupted.

Even after a call for the Previous Question (Section 20) brings a matter under discussion to an immediate vote, from the time of ordering the Previous Question until the moment of taking the last vote under it, it still is in order to move to Lay on the Table the matter that was being discussed.

The motion to Lay [a matter] on the Table has high privileges. It outranks every debatable question, is undebatable itself, and requires only a majority vote for adoption. An organization needs such a motion so that it can instantly put aside certain business and attend to more urgent matters. However, in parliamentary law, the reasoning is that every motion that suppresses a matter for the session should be open to free debate (see Section 35) unless such debate is limited or closed by at least a two-thirds vote (see Section 39).

In meetings that last only a few hours, a bare majority may table an objectionable motion and thereby suppress it without permitting debate; however, this is an abuse of the motion that often disturbs the harmony of voluntary groups.

The motion to Lay [a subject] on the Table has high privileges because the assumption is that a matter will be set aside only temporarily. Although the motion is valuable when used legitimately, it should require a two-thirds vote if it's going to be used habitually to suppress other motions. The following example suggests a partial remedy for the unfair use of the motion.

> *Example:* If you introduce a resolution and then are cut off from speaking by another motion to Lay on the Table the matter you proposed, you should follow this procedure: Immediately claim the floor, which you had and to which you were entitled (see Section 2), and make your speech. Often people who move for a question to be tabled are in such a hurry that they fail to address the chair and obtain the floor properly. In such case, you should quickly address the chair, making a point of order—you were the first one to address the chair and the member who interrupted you failed to do so and, not having the floor, isn't entitled to make a motion. Hence it's your right to continue. An alert chair will realize what has happened and act immediately as shown here:
>
> *Mr. Boyle:* Therefore, I propose that . . .
>
> *Mrs. Solomon (interrupting):* I move that we table this question.
>
> *Chair:* Mrs. Solomon has not been recognized by the chair. Mr. Boyle, you still have the floor. Please continue.

Since motions that are tabled are merely put aside temporarily, if enough members of the majority opinion leave, the minority could all stay until the moment of final adjournment and by then might be in the majority. They could then take up and pass any resolutions on the table.

A safer and fairer procedure, however, would be to make an Objection to the Consideration of the Question (Section 15). This would assume that the matter is so objectionable that it would be best not to allow even its introducer to speak on it. But if there already had been debate on the subject, you couldn't object to its consideration.

You could also make a motion for the Previous Question (Section 20); if that motion would pass, it immediately would bring the matter to a vote. An objection to considering a motion and a call for the Previous Question are both legitimate ways of finding out if a group really wants to discuss a subject. Since the motions require a two-thirds vote, no one should object to them.

The motion to Lay [a question] on the Table can't be applied to more than the matter that's before the assembly at the time and whatever properly pertains to it. Therefore, it would be improper to lay aside committee reports (two or more) or unfinished business in general (all of the applicable subjects) when that part of the meeting is reached. Possible alternatives would be to move to Suspend the Rules (Section 18), a motion that requires a two-thirds vote, or to table each successive, *individual* report as it comes up for action.

Section 20. The Previous Question

The *Previous Question* is a technical name for a motion that gives one the wrong impression because it has nothing to do with the subject considered previously. To demand the Previous Question is to move that debate on a matter cease and that the assembly immediately vote on the *pending* motion(s). Therefore, if a chair asks, "Shall the main question be now put [to a vote]?" he or she really means, "Shall the *pending* motion be now put to a vote?" (See Section 37 for the motion to Limit Debate.)

A call for the Previous Question, which is not debatable, takes precedence over every debatable question (see Section 35). But it yields to incidental questions (see Section 8) and privileged questions (see Section 9) and to the motion to Lay [a subject] on the Table (Section 19). After someone demands the Previous Question and until final action on it is taken, you may move to Adjourn (Section 11) or move that the pending motion be tabled.

The call for the Previous Question can't be amended or have any other subsidiary motion (see Section 7) applied to it. But *it* can be applied to, or used together with, Questions of Privilege (Section 12) as well as to any other debatable motion. You could, therefore, submit a resolution and at the same time move for the Previous Question.

The call for the Previous Question may be reconsidered but not after being partially executed. To be adopted, it requires a two-thirds vote. A single vote is taken in reconsidering the Previous Question. The chair would ask:

Will the assembly reconsider the motion ordering the Previous Question?

If the vote is in favor of reconsidering the call for the Previous Question, the pending motion is free of it. Since the call for the Previous Question is itself undebatable and also ends the debate on the pending motion, members wouldn't vote to reconsider it unless they wanted to reopen the debate.

> In the House the motion for the Previous Question must be seconded by a majority (to avoid the "yeas and nays" [see Section 38]), and then it can be adopted by a majority vote; in the Senate this is not allowed. In the House the motion is sometimes called the "gag law" since a bare majority can adopt it. The right of debate, however, should be considered an established rule in every deliberative body, one that can't be changed except by a vote that can suspend any rule (see Section 39).

When someone calls for the Previous Question, and the call is seconded, the chair immediately asks a question such as this:

Shall the main [pending] question be now put?

Are you ready for the question?

A vote is then taken on the call for the Previous Question. If the motion fails, the discussion on the original subject (pending motion) continues as though the motion calling for the Previous Question had never been made. If the motion passes, though, its effect is as follows:

- The effect of passing a call for the Previous Question (except when motions to Amend and to Commit are pending) is to close the debate on the original subject instantly and to require that the assembly vote on the pending matter. (But after the debate is closed on a question reported from a committee, the person reporting it may make a closing speech. See Section 34.) After the assembly has voted, the business before the assembly stands exactly as if the vote on the pending motion had been taken in the usual way (without a demand for the Previous Question having forced the vote). If the vote on the call for the Previous Question is reconsidered (see Section 27), the original matter (pending question) is released from the Previous Question and is again open to debate.

- The effect when either of the motions to Amend (Section 23) or to Commit (Section 22) is pending is to cut off debate and force a vote not only on those motions but also on the pending motion to be amended or committed. If you think of the motions to Amend and to Commit as inseparable from the main (pending) question to be amended or committed, there is really only one question. Then the effect of adopting the Previous Question is simply to cut off debate and force the assembly to vote on that one pending question. This may be the easiest way to view this matter since it makes it as simple as adopting an order closing debate (see Section 37). The motion to Close Debate would have the same privileges (and therefore the same complications) as the call for the Previous Question.

The chair puts to a vote these various motions in order of precedence, beginning with the motion that was made last. The Previous Question is not exhausted (concluded) until votes have been taken on all of the pending motions (to Amend, to Commit, and so on) or until there has been a vote to refer the matter to a committee. If one of the votes is reconsidered before the Previous Question is exhausted, the fact that the call for the Previous Question is pending means that the motion being reconsidered can't be debated.

The motion calling for the Previous Question may be limited to or concern only the pending amendment; if the motion passes, then, debate is closed only on the amendment. After the amendment is voted on, the original question (the pending motion that was being amended) is again open to debate and further amendment. Acceptable forms of the motion calling for the Previous Question are as follows:

Shall the question be now put on the amendment?

Shall debate close now and a vote be taken on the amendment?

In the same manner, you can make a motion to amend an amendment.

The object of the call for the Previous Question is to bring the assembly to an immediate vote on the original subject being considered without further debate. For other ways of closing debate, see Sections 37 and 38.

An Appeal (Section 14) from the decision of the chair is undebatable (see Section 35) if it's made after someone has moved for the Previous Question and before final action is taken.

The following examples illustrate the effect of the call for the Previous Question in various circumstances:

Example: **Suppose that a question is before the assembly and someone makes another motion to Amend it. Then imagine that someone else moves to Postpone [the pending question] to a Certain Time (Section 21). If the Previous Question is then ordered, it stops the debate and forces a vote on the postponement. When that vote is taken, the effect of the Previous Question is exhausted (no longer applies). But if the assembly refuses to postpone the subject, the debate on the amendment is resumed.**

Example: **Suppose that a subject under consideration is interrupted by a Question of Privilege (Section 12) and that someone moves to Refer (Section 22) the Question of Privilege to a com-**

mittee. If the Previous Question is then ordered, it brings the assembly to a vote, first on the motion to Refer and, if that one fails, next on the Question of Privilege. After the Question of Privilege is voted on, the Previous Question is exhausted, and consideration of the original subject is resumed.

Example: Suppose that while an amendment to a motion is pending someone makes another motion to Refer the matter to a committee. Then someone moves to Amend the referral motion by giving the committee instructions. In addition to the original motion, therefore, two other motions have been made—to Amend and to Refer. If someone now calls for the Previous Question, it will apply to all of the motions as though there is just one. The chair will immediately put the matter to a vote in this order:

- First, on the committee's instructions.

- Second, on the motion to Refer; if this is adopted the subject is referred to the committee, and the effect of the Previous question is exhausted.

- Third, if the motion to Refer fails, on the amendment.

- Finally, on the original question.

Much of the confusion about the Previous Question has been caused by the great changes in this motion since its conception in the English Parliament. There it was intended and is still used to suppress the main question (not the debate). It was first used in 1604 and was intended to be applied only to delicate questions. The form then was "Shall the main question be put?" If there was a negative response, the main question was dismissed for that session. The present form is "Shall the main question be now put?" At first, if the response was negative, the question was dismissed only until after the ensuing debate. Now it's dismissed for the day. The motion calling for the Previous Question could be debated, but once it was voted on, it prevented any discussion of the main question. If the vote was yes (to put the main question to a vote), the main question was immediately put to a vote. If the vote was no (not to put it to a vote), the main question was dismissed for the day.

Congress has changed the idea of the Previous Question. Whereas in England the one who moves for the Previous Question votes against it, in the United States the mover votes for it. In 1805 Congress made the Previous Question undebatable. In 1860 Congress allowed the consideration of a subject to be resumed if the Previous Question didn't pass. At first its effect was to cut off all motions except the main question, and a vote was immediately taken on it. In 1840 this was changed to bring the House to a vote first on pending amendments and then on the main question. In 1848 the rule was changed again to bring the House to a vote on the motion to Commit (if any), then on amendments reported by a committee (if any), next on pending amendments, and finally on the main question. In 1860 Congress decided that the only effect of the Previous Question, if a motion to postpone were pending, should be to bring the House to a direct vote on the postponement. This would prevent the Previous Question from cutting off any pending motion. The Previous Question is now a simple motion to close debate and proceed to voting. (But to stop someone from introducing an improper or useless subject in an ordinary group, one should object to its consideration [see Section 15] when first introduced. This motion is very similar to the English version of the Previous Question.)

Section 21. To Postpone to a Certain Time

The motion to Postpone to a Certain Time a particular matter takes precedence over a motion to Commit (Section 22), Amend (Section 23), or Postpone [it] Indefinitely (Section 24). But it yields to any incidental question (see Section 8) or privileged question (see Section 9), to the motion to Lay [the matter] on the Table (Section 19), or to a call for the Previous Question (Section 20).

The motion to Postpone [a matter] to a Certain Time can be amended by altering the time. Also, the Previous Question can be applied to the motion to Postpone to a Certain Time without affecting any other pending motions. The motion to Postpone [a matter] to a Certain Time allows very limited debate (see Section 35). Such debate, however, must not delve into the merits of the subject any more than is necessary for the assembly to make a judgment about the postponement.

The effect of the motion to Postpone [a matter] to a Certain Time is to postpone the entire subject to a specified time. Until that time, it can't be taken up unless there's a two-thirds vote (see Section 13) to do so. When the specified time arrives, it may be taken up in preference to everything else except privileged questions (see Section 9).

When several matters are postponed to different times but are not brought up at those times, the subjects eventually must be considered in the order of the times to which they were postponed. If you propose another time, it must not be beyond the *current* session of the assembly (see Section 42), unless the organization meets regularly. In that case, it must not be beyond the end of the next *regular* session, at which time the subject would come up with the unfinished business and thus would take precedence over new business on that day (see Section 44).

If members want to hold an adjourned (continued) meeting to consider a special subject, someone should move to Fix the Time to Which to Adjourn (Section 10) rather than make a motion to postpone the subject to that day. (In Congress a motion can't be postponed to the next session, although it is customary in ordinary groups to do this.)

Section 22. To Commit or Refer

The motion to Commit or Refer a subject to a committee takes precedence over the motions to Amend (Section 23) it or to Postpone [it] Indefinitely (Section 24). (If a subject was previously committed, the proper term is to *Recommit*.) But the motion yields to any incidental question (see Section 8) or any privileged question (see Section 9). It also yields to the motions to Lay [a matter] on the Table (Section 19), to a call for the Previous Question (Section 20), and to Postpone [a matter] to a Certain Time (Section 21).

The motion to Commit or Refer a matter can be amended by altering the committee or giving the committee instructions. Also, it is debatable, and it opens to debate (see Section 35) the merits of the matter to be committed.

A common form of the motion is as follows:

I move to refer _____ to a committee.

When different committees are proposed, they should be voted on in the following order:

- Committee of the whole (see Section 32)

- Standing committee

- Special (or select) committee

The number of people to serve on a committee is usually decided without the formality of a motion, as is also the case with filling in blanks (see Section 23). The chair would ask something such as this:

How many shall there be on the committee?

A motion is then made for each number suggested, starting with the smallest number. But the number of members and kind of committee need not be decided until after the vote to Refer the subject to a committee has taken place.

With a select committee, when the motion does not state how to appoint it and there is no standing rule on the subject, the chair will ask how the committee should be appointed. This matter is usually decided informally. Sometimes the chair appoints the members, simply naming them without any vote on them.

The committee could also be nominated by the chair or members of the assembly. No one, however, should nominate more than one person except by general consent. Then the nominees are all voted on together unless there are more people nominated than the number proposed for the committee; in that case, each one would have to be voted on individually.

A committee formed for some activity (such as making arrangements for a building dedication) generally should be small. Also, no one should be on it who is opposed to the proposed action. Any such opponent who is appointed should ask to be excused. A committee formed for purposes of investigation or deliberation, though, must have all parties (that is, those representing all sides of an issue) on it to provide for thorough discussion in the committee and to avoid later unpleasant debates in the assembly.

In ordinary groups, the careful selection of committee members representing all views of delicate and troublesome questions will help to limit debates to the committee itself (see Section 28).

Section 23. To Amend

The motion to Amend another motion takes precedence only over the motion to be amended. It yields to any other subsidiary motion (see Section 7) except one to Postpone [a matter] Indefinitely (Section 24), any incidental motion (see Section 8), or any privileged motion (see Section 9). It can be applied to all motions except the eight motions listed later in this section, which can't be amended. The motion to Amend can itself even be amended, although such amendment of an amendment can't be altered further.

An amendment might be inconsistent with another amendment already adopted, and it also could be in direct conflict with the spirit of the original motion. It must have a direct bearing on the subject of the original motion.

Example: A motion for a vote of thanks could be amended by striking out *thanks* and inserting the word *censure*.

Example: A motion condemning certain customs could be amended by adding other customs.

An amendment may take any of the following forms:

- To "add" or "insert" certain words or paragraphs.

- To "strike out" certain words or paragraphs. If that motion fails to pass, another amendment is possible. (Previously, the form for this motion was "Shall these words stand as part of the resolution?" Now, in the United States, it's treated the same as any other motion.)

- To "strike out certain words and insert others." This motion can't be divided. If it fails to pass, another one can be offered to strike out the same words and insert different words. (Rule 18 of the Senate, however, states that in amending a motion to strike out A and insert B, the amendment is considered as two questions, and the amendment to the first part on words to be removed takes precedence.)

- To "substitute" another resolution or paragraph on the same subject for the one that's pending.

- To divide a motion into two or more motions, as the mover specifies, to get a separate vote on a specific point(s) (see Section 4).

If you want to insert a paragraph, it should be worded exactly as the proponents want it to read—*before* voting on it. Once it has been inserted, it's too late: It can't be struck out or amended, except by adding to it.

The same thing is true concerning words to be inserted in a resolution. Once they're inserted, they can't be taken out except by making a motion to strike out (1) the entire paragraph or (2) some portion of it that would make the motion entirely different from what it would be with the words inserted. In other words, once a group has voted to insert certain words in a resolution, it's not in order to make another motion involving exactly the same question that was just decided. The only way to bring it up again is to move to Reconsider (Section 27) the vote that was taken to insert the words.

Filling in Blanks. Amendments about filling in blanks differ from others in that members may propose, without a second, different numbers to fill in. These proposals, however, are not treated as amendments of one another; they're considered to be independent propositions that must be voted on successively.

The correct order for voting is that the smallest sum and the longest time are put first. (The Senate follows this practice of not treating the proposals as amendments of one another and also gives preference to the smallest sum. The House, though, treats filling in blanks the same as other amendments.)

Nominations. As is the case with filling in blanks, with nominations a second nomination is not considered to be an amendment of the first; rather, it's an independent motion to be voted on if the first one fails to receive a majority vote.

Any number of nominations may be made, and the chair should announce each name as it's given. The nominations should then be voted on in the order announced by the chair until someone is elected. This requires a majority vote unless the organization's bylaws specify a different number.

If paragraphs in an amendment are numbered, the numbers are treated as merely marginal notations, not part of the paragraph content. They should be corrected (if necessary), therefore, by the secretary, or clerk, without making any motion to Amend (to correct the number).

Amending an organization's rules of order or bylaws or its charter, articles of incorporation, or constitution would require first giving previous notice to the members and then a two-thirds vote for the amendment to pass (see also Section 48; see Section 45; for instructions on amending the reports of committees or propositions with several paragraphs, see Section 31; on amending the minutes of meetings, see Section 41; on the proper form for making a motion to Amend, see Section 65). These motions can't be amended:

- To Adjourn, when unqualified (Section 11)
- To call for the Orders of the Day (Section 13)
- All incidental questions (Section 8)
- To Lay [a subject] on the Table (Section 19)
- To call for the Previous Question (Section 20)
- To Amend an Amendment (Section 23)
- To Postpone [a matter] Indefinitely (Section 24)
- To Reconsider a matter (Section 27)

The following guidelines apply to amendments:

- A resolution is amended by altering the words of the resolution.
- An amendment is amended by altering the words of the amendment—that is, by altering the words being inserted or taken out.
- The *form* of a motion to Amend can't be amended; that is, you can't substitute an entirely new or different motion. For example, a motion to *adopt* a resolution can't be amended to substitute a motion to *reject* the resolution (that would alter the *form,* not merely the words, of the resolution). For example:
  - A motion to "strike out A" can't be amended by adding "and insert B" (which would be read as "strike out A and insert B"); that would be another *form* of amendment and not merely an alteration of A.
  - A motion to "insert B before the word C" in a resolution can't be amended by substituting another resolution for the one pending, thus chang-

ing the *form* of the amendment and not simply
altering B.

- A motion to "insert B before the word C" can't be
  amended by adding "and D before the word E";
  the only thing that can be altered in the pending
  amendment is B; the other words are those that are
  necessary to describe what is being proposed to do
  with B.

- If a pending amendment is to "insert A, B, C, and
  D before F," it's in order to apply any form of
  amendment to A, B, C, and D. But no amendment
  is in order that's not confined simply to altering the
  words A, B, C, and D.

- When a member wants to make a motion for an
  amendment that's not in order at the time but affects the pending question, that person should state
  his or her intention to offer another amendment if
  the pending amendment is voted down. Then those
  who favor that member's alternative amendment
  have a chance to vote down the pending amendment, paving the way for the new one to be offered.

Section 24. To Postpone Indefinitely

The motion to Postpone [a subject] Indefinitely takes
precedence only over the pending motion, the one to be
postponed (see Section 6). It yields to any other subsidiary
motion (see Section 7) except one to Amend (Section 23),
any incidental motion (see Section 8), or any privileged
motion (see Section 9). It can be applied only to a principal
question or a Question of Privilege (Section 12).

The motion to Postpone [a matter] Indefinitely can't
be amended. Also, it opens to debate the entire matter
proposed for postponement. If the Previous Question
(Section 20) is ordered when the motion to Postpone
Indefinitely is pending, the Previous Question applies
only to the postponement and doesn't affect the original subject.

The effect of a motion to Postpone [something] Indefinitely is to remove the matter from the assembly

for that session (see Section 42). A vote to Postpone Indefinitely has the same effect as a negative vote on the original subject. But it's useful when the opposition doubts its strength. Even if opponents are defeated on the matter of postponement, then, they still will have a chance to fight the original question.

Miscellaneous Motions

Section 25. To Rescind

The motion to Rescind is used when an assembly wants to annul some prior action and it's too late to reconsider (see Section 27) the vote on it. This motion has no privileges but has the same importance as a new resolution. Any action of a group can be rescinded regardless of the time that has elapsed.

In rare cases, when a group wants not only to rescind some action but to express very strong disapproval of it, it could vote to rescind the objectionable action and remove it from the record. You could do this by crossing out the undesirable words, or drawing a line around them, and writing across the words "Expunged by order of the assembly . . . ," adding the date of the order.

Section 26. Renewal of a Motion

Once a principal motion (see Section 6) or amendment has been acted on by a group, it can't be taken up again at the same session (see Section 42) except by making a motion to Reconsider (Section 27) the vote on it. Moreover, once that motion to Reconsider has been acted on, it, too, can't be repeated in regard to the same motion—unless the motion was amended when it was previously reconsidered.

However, a correction of the minutes (see Section 41) can be made without a motion to Reconsider at the same or any subsequent session. A motion to Rescind (Section 25) can also be made at the same or any subsequent session. The motion to Adjourn (Section 11) can be renewed if in the meantime the debate has progressed or if any business has since been transacted.

Generally, if any motion is introduced that alters the state of affairs, this means that you can renew (1) any privileged or incidental motion (except for a motion calling for Orders of the Day [Section 13] or to Suspend the Rules [Section 18]) or (2) any subsidiary motion (except for an amendment). The reason that it's possible to renew such motions is that the real question before the assembly is then different.

> *Example:* Suppose that a motion for a matter to Lay on the Table (Section 19) fails and someone then moves to Refer (Section 22) the matter to a committee. It would then be in order to move again that the subject be tabled. Such a motion would not be in order, though, if you waited until the motion to Refer failed. If it failed, the motion would return to its previous status. Therefore, if a subject has been taken from the table or if an objection to considering it has been voted down, you can't move to table it because that would involve essentially the same question that the assembly just decided.

When a subject has been referred to a committee that reports at the *same* meeting, the matter is then treated as if it has been introduced for the first time. Also, a motion that has been withdrawn in a meeting obviously hasn't been acted on, so it can then be renewed.

Section 27. Reconsider

You may move to Reconsider a vote and have the motion entered on the record at any time—except while another motion is before the assembly—including (1) when someone else has the floor, (2) while the assembly is voting on a motion to Adjourn (Section 11), (3) during the day when the motion of concern has been acted on, or (4) on the next succeeding day.

If the vote on some motion isn't reconsidered on the day the vote was taken or the next succeeding day, the vote can't be reconsidered at the next (later) meeting. The proper course then would be to *renew* the motion if it previously failed or to Rescind (Section 25) it if it was previously adopted.

The motion to Reconsider a vote must be made by a member who voted with the prevailing side (whether it was for or against), unless the vote was by ballot, in which case votes are secret. However, anyone can second the motion. (In Congress anyone can move to Reconsider something unless the vote was taken by "yeas and nays" [Section 38], in which case the above rule applies.)

If a motion fails to pass for lack of a two-thirds vote, the move to Reconsider the vote must be made by the person who voted against the motion. In this case, someone who voted against it would be on the prevailing side.

A motion to Reconsider the vote on a subsidiary motion (see Section 7) takes precedence over the main motion. But it yields to incidental motions (see Section 8) and privileged questions (see Section 9) except for the call for Orders of the Day (Section 13).

The motion to Reconsider a matter can be applied to the vote on every other motion except one to Adjourn (Section 11) or to Suspend the Rules (Section 18) and except for an affirmative vote on the motion to Lay [a matter] on the Table or to Take [a matter] from the Table (Section 19), as well as a vote electing someone to office who is present and doesn't decline.

One should not reconsider an affirmative vote on the motion to Lay [a matter] on the Table because the same results can be obtained by making a motion to Take [the matter] from the Table. For the same reason, one wouldn't reconsider an affirmative vote to Take [the matter] from the Table.

No motion may be reconsidered twice unless it was amended after reconsidering it the first time. The minutes, however, may be corrected any number of times without making a motion to Reconsider the vote approving them. If an amendment to a motion has been adopted (or rejected) and then if a vote is taken on the motion as amended, you may not reconsider the vote on the amendment until you have first reconsidered the vote on the original motion. Also, if the motion for the Previous Question (Section 20) has been partially executed, it may not be reconsidered.

If something was done that an assembly *can't* reverse—something done by vote—that vote can't be re-considered. A motion to Reconsider a vote can't be amended. It may or may not be debated, depending on whether the motion that's being reconsidered may or may not be debated (see Section 35).

When a motion to Reconsider something is debatable, it also opens to discussion the entire subject that's being reconsidered. But if the Previous Question (Section 20) is ordered while a motion to Reconsider is pending, the Previous Question affects only the motion to Reconsider, not the entire subject being reconsidered.

The motion to Reconsider can itself be tabled (see Section 19), in which case the reconsideration, like any other matter that was set aside, can later be taken from the table. But it has no privileges. When a motion to Reconsider is tabled, it doesn't carry with it the pending measure (the one being reconsidered).

The effect of making a motion to Reconsider is to suspend all action that would have been necessary under the original motion until the members act on the reconsideration. But (with one exception) if the motion to Reconsider the matter is not called up for a vote during the session, its effect terminates with *that* session (see Section 42).

In Congress a member in charge of an important bill usually moves to Reconsider the vote on it as soon as it passes. At the same time the member usually moves that the motion to Reconsider be laid on the table. If the motion to Lay [the reconsideration] on the Table is adopted, the decision is considered final, since the large number of bills awaiting action means that it will not likely be taken up again, except by a two-thirds vote. This isn't true in ordinary groups, however, and there is no good reason in this case to violate the principle that only one motion can be made at a time.

An exception applies to a group having regular meetings as often as weekly or monthly when there's no adjourned meeting (no continuation of the meeting at which the move to Reconsider was made) scheduled for another day. Then the effect of making the motion to Reconsider does not end until the close of the *next* succeeding session.

The move to Reconsider a subsidiary motion (see Section 7) or an incidental motion (see Section 8) must be acted on immediately, since otherwise the members couldn't act on the main (pending) motion. An exception occurs when the vote to be reconsidered had the effect of removing the entire subject before the assembly.

> *Example:* Suppose that a motion to Postpone [a matter] Indefinitely is voted down, indicating that the group wants to consider the subject in question. If someone moves to Reconsider that last vote, the reconsideration has to be acted on immediately, as explained above, or, in effect, the whole subject will be removed, without any possible benefit to the assembly. If you want to stop a temporary majority from adopting a resolution, the proper course is to wait until the assembly finally acts on the resolution and then move to Reconsider the vote on it. But suppose that a motion to Postpone [the matter] Indefinitely passes; then the subject is removed from before the assembly. In that case, the reconsideration can be held over to another day, and other business can be transacted in the meantime.

Although the motion to Reconsider is very highly privileged in regard to having it entered in the minutes (with action on it delayed until it is called up later), the reconsideration of a matter must not interfere with the discussion of another subject presently before the assembly. As soon as the current subject is disposed of, however, the reconsideration, if called up, takes precedence over everything except the motions to Adjourn (Section 11) and to Fix the Time to Which to Adjourn (Section 10).

When a reconsideration has been brought before the assembly for action, it can be treated like any other motion and can be held over as unfinished business. As long as the effect of the motion for reconsideration lasts (that is, as long as it hasn't yet been disposed of), anyone may call up the motion to Reconsider and have it acted on. An exception to this is when its effect extends beyond the meeting at which the motion to Reconsider is made; then no one but the mover can call it up at the next meeting.

The effect of adopting the motion to Reconsider a vote is to put the original motion before the assembly again in the exact position it held before it was voted on. Hence no one can debate the matter to be reconsidered who previously has exhausted his or her right to debate (see Section 34) that question. A person's only recourse, then, is to discuss the original subject while the motion to Reconsider is before the assembly.

When a vote taken under the order of the Previous Question (Section 20) is reconsidered, the original motion is then free of the Previous Question and is again open to debate the amendment. This is true as long as the Previous Question was acted on (exhausted)—by votes taken on all of the subjects it concerned—before the motion to Reconsider was made.

A reconsideration needs only a majority vote. This is true regardless of the vote needed (such as two-thirds) to adopt the original motion that was reconsidered. (For reconsidering a vote in committee, see Section 28.)

In the English Parliament, once a vote is taken, it can't be reconsidered. But in the U.S. Congress, members may move to Reconsider a vote on the same or the succeeding day. After the close of the last day for making the motion, anyone may call up the motion to Reconsider. Therefore, this motion can't delay action more than two days, and the effect of the motion, if not acted on, terminates with the session. There seems to be no reason or good precedent for allowing two persons, by moving to Reconsider, to suspend for any length of time all action under resolutions adopted by the assembly. Yet when the delay is very short, the advantages of reconsideration outweigh the disadvantages.

When a permanent organization has weekly or monthly meetings and when, usually, only a small percentage of the members are present, it seems best to permit a reconsideration to hold over to another meeting so that a larger proportion of the group will be aware of what action is about to be taken.

Steps can be taken to prevent someone from using the motion to Reconsider a vote to defeat a measure that can't be deferred until the next regular meeting; in case the group adjourns until another day, the reconsideration will not hold over beyond that session. This allows sufficient delay to notify the group about the motion; if the question requires immediate action, the delay can't extend beyond the day to which the meeting adjourns (is continued). The rule is that the meeting must be held on *another day* to prevent the defeat of the whole object of the reconsideration by an immediate adjournment merely until a few minutes later.

When meetings are only quarterly or annual, a group should be properly represented at each meeting. The group's best interests are served by following the practice of Congress and letting the effect of the reconsideration end with the session.

Article IV. Committees and Informal Action

Section 28. Committees

Large assemblies usually have committees do the preliminary work of preparing some matter for their action. These committees may be standing or select committees or a committee of the whole (see Section 32).

- *Standing committees* are appointed for a particular session (see Section 42) or for some definite time such as one year.

- *Select committees* are appointed for a special purpose.

- A *committee of the whole* consists of the entire assembly. (For the method of appointing committees of the whole, see Section 32; for other committees, see Section 22.)

A committee (except a committee of the whole; see Section 32) in turn may appoint a subcommittee.

The first person named to be on a committee is the committee chair. In the absence of that person, the next-named member becomes the committee chair and so on. The committee, however, has the authority to elect another chair if it wishes, unless the assembly has already appointed a committee chair.

The secretary, or clerk, of the assembly should advise the committee chair, or another member of the committee, of the appointment of the committee and give (1) the names of the members, (2) the matter referred to them, and (3) any instructions from the assembly.

An *ex-officio member* of a committee or board is a member by virtue of holding some office. But if the office isn't controlled by the organization, there's no distinction between the ex-officio member and other members.

If the ex-officio member is *not* under the authority of the organizaation, he or she has all of the privileges but none of the obligations of membership. This is similar to the status of a governor of a state who is acting ex-officio as manager or trustee of a private academy.

Sometimes the bylaws specify that the group's president shall be ex-officio a member of every committee. The intent in such cases is to *allow,* not require, the president to act as a member of the various committees. In determining a quorum, then, the president should not be counted as a member of the committee. The president would be a member of any committee only by virtue of a special rule, unless the assembly would appoint him or her as a member.

Once the committee is formed, its chair should call the members together. If there's a quorum (a majority; see Section 43), the chair would then read, or have read, the entire matter or resolution(s) referred to the committee.

After reading each paragraph, the committee chair should pause to allow amendments to be offered. After any amendments to a particular paragraph are voted on, the chair would read the next paragraph and so on. The committee can only vote on amendments; it can't vote to adopt the entire matter referred to it by the assembly.

The resolutions, however, might originate in a committee rather than in the assembly. Then they would be prepared by a committee member(s) or a subcommittee. Nevertheless, the committee would still handle (read) the draft of any resolution paragraph by paragraph and vote on amendments in the same manner.

Any vote would concern amendments only, however; the committee would not vote to adopt each paragraph. Rather, at the end of all votes on amendments, it would vote to adopt the entire report (see Section 31). A preamble (if any) is considered last.

When the report *originates* in a committee, then, all amendments are incorporated into the report. But when resolutions are *referred* to a committee by the assembly, the committee must not alter the text. Instead, it must submit to the assembly the original paper intact with the committee's amendments (which may be in the form of a substitute, such as other resolutions or paragraphs; see Section 23) written on a separate sheet of paper.

A committee is a miniature assembly that must meet to transact business. Any two members can call for a meeting if the committee chair is absent or declines to call a meeting. Usually, one of the members is appointed as clerk, or secretary.

When a quorum is present, a majority of the members at the meeting must agree in order for something to form part of the committee's report. The minority, however, may submit its views in writing (together or each member separately). But minority reports can be acted on only by voting to substitute one of them for the report of the committee (see Section 30).

The rules of the assembly, as much as possible, also

apply in a committee. The committee chair usually takes the most active part in the discussions and work. A motion in a committee, however, does not require a second, and (except in large committees) a member need not stand while speaking.

Although small committees may dispense with motions, they should always take a vote to establish exactly what has been decided. A reconsideration (see Section 27) of a vote is allowed, regardless of the time elapsed, only when every member who voted with the majority is present when someone moves to Reconsider the vote.

Both English common parliamentary law and the rules of Congress prohibit a committee from reconsidering a vote. But if this rule were strictly enforced in ordinary committees it would hinder rather than help efforts to transact business. The rule allowing a reconsideration seems more just and appropriate for ordinary committees. The privilege won't be abused as long as everyone who voted with the majority is present when the move to Reconsider occurs.

When a committee is finished with the business assigned to it, someone makes a motion for the committee to Rise and for the chair (or another member more familiar with the subject) to report to the assembly. In a committee, the motion to Rise is the same as the motion to Adjourn (Section 11) in an assembly. As soon as the assembly receives the committee's report (see Section 30), the committee ceases to exist, unless it's a standing committee.

A committee has no power to punish its members for disorderly conduct, but it can report the pertinent facts to the assembly. It can't, however, allude to what has occurred except by a report of the committee to the assembly or by general consent.

When a committee adjourns without setting a time for the next meeting, it's called together again in the same way as with its first meeting. When a committee adjourns to meet at another time, it's not necessary (but is a good idea) to notify absent members of the adjourned (continued) meeting.

Section 29. Forms of Committee Reports

A common form of wording the introduction to a committee report is illustrated in these examples:

> *Standing Committee:* The committee on _____ respectfully reports [*or* "respectfully submits the following report"] . . . [*followed by the report comments*].

> *Select or Special Committee:* The committee [*or* "Your committee" *or* "The undersigned, a committee"] to which was referred _____, having considered the same, respectfully reports . . . [*followed by the report comments*].

> *Minority Report:* The undersigned, a minority of a committee to which we referred, . . . [*followed by the report comments*].

Unlike the minority report, the majority report is the report of the committee and should not be described as the report of the majority.

Although it is not required, a report may conclude by stating the following:

Respectfully submitted.

A committee report is usually signed only by the chair of the committee. If the matter is of great importance, however, it should be signed by every member who concurs in the report.

Although a report is not usually dated or addressed, it may have a heading such as this:

Report of the Finance Committee of the YPA on Renting a Hall

The report would usually close or be accompanied by a formal resolution covering all of its recommendations. The adoption of the report (see Section 31) would then have the effect of adopting *all* of the resolutions necessary to carry out the committee's recommendations. The following example, however, illustrates an exception to this effect:

> *Example:* **Suppose that a committee report on a certain subject also stated: "Your committee thinks that the conduct of Mrs. Mulligan at the last meeting was so serious that it recommends she be expelled from the society." The adoption of the committee's report by the governing assembly would not have the effect of expelling Mrs. Mulligan.**

A committee may be able to carry out its assigned task just by reporting a resolution. In that case, the resolution alone is submitted in writing.

Section 30. Reception of Reports

When a committee is ready to report, the committee chair or someone appointed to make the report informs the assembly. The person selected would indicate to the assembly that the committee to which a particular subject or paper was referred had directed him or her to report thereon or to report it with or without amendment, as the case may be. That person or another member might then move that the report be *received* at the time or at another specified time.

Sometimes errors in procedure occur at this stage, as shown in these examples:

> *Example:* **A very common error occurs after a committee report has been read to the assembly. Someone may move that the report be *received* then. But the fact that it has been read indicates that the assembly has already received it.**

> *Example:* **A less common but dangerous mistake concerns the adoption of a report. A group may vote to accept a report (equivalent to**

adopting it; see Section 31) when it means only to consider the report and, after that, move for adoption.

Example: Another error involves the discharge of a committee. Someone may move that "the report be adopted and *the committee be discharged then"* when the committee has already reported in full and its report has already been received. By that time, therefore, the committee no longer exists anyway. On the other hand, if the committee had made only a partial report or a progress report, it would be in order to move to discharge the committee from further consideration of the subject.

Usually, an assembly dispenses with the formality of a vote to *receive* a committee report, and the time when the report will be given is settled by general consent. But if anyone objects, a formal motion is necessary. When it's time for the assembly to receive the report, the chair of the committee (or other member) reads it (without leaving his or her seat) before handing it to the clerk, or secretary, of the assembly. It will then lie on the table (see Section 19) until the assembly is ready to consider it.

After the committee chair (or other person) reads the report, it's a good idea for him or her to move that the assembly accept (or adopt) it or to make whatever other motion will carry out the committee's recommendations.

If a report consists of a paper with amendments, the committee chair (or other person) would read the amendments along with enough of the related part in the paper to be understandable. The person reading would explain the alterations and given reasons for the amendments as each one came up until he or she had gone through all of them. When a report is very long, it's usually not read until the assembly is ready to consider it (see Section 31).

Once a report has been *received,* whether or not it has been read, the committee is thereby dissolved and can act no further unless there's a vote to Recommit (Section 22) the matter (send it back to the committee). If the report is recommitted, all parts not agreed to by the assembly are ignored by the committee as though the report had never been made.

If a member(s) wants to submit a minority report(s), the assembly usually receives it right after receiving the committee report. But the assembly can't act on the minority report unless someone moves to substitute it for the committee report.

Section 31. Adoption of Reports

When an assembly is ready to consider a report, someone should move to *adopt, accept,* or *agree to* the report. You can use any of those terms to accomplish the same thing. When the motion is carried, it has the effect of making the committee's work become the acts of the assembly just as if the assembly had done the work without a committee. Therefore, if the committee's report has formal resolutions, the assembly adopts those resolutions. (But when a committee's report is only informational, there is no need to take any action after it has been read.)

The motions to adopt, accept, or agree to a report generally are used indiscriminately. But even though they all have the same effect, it would be better to vary the motion according to the character of the report.

> *Example:* Suppose that the report contains only a statement of opinion or facts. The best form, then, is to *accept* the report.

> *Example:* Suppose that the report contains a statement of opinion and facts but also concludes with resolutions or orders. The best form, then, is to *agree to* the resolution or to *adopt* the orders. If either of these motions is carried, the effect is to adopt the entire report.

To *adopt* the report is the most common of the motions in ordinary groups. It's used regardless of the character of the report. Although the effect of the motion to adopt a report is generally understood, that's not always the case with the term *to accept.* (See Section 30; see also Section 30 for common errors in acting on reports; see Section 29 for the way in which the form of a report influences its adoption.)

After someone moves either to accept or adopt a report, the report is open to amendment. The matter then stands before the assembly as if there had been no committee and as if the subject had just been introduced by the motion of the member who was reporting.

One should be especially careful with an annual report of an executive committee or a board that's published as its report. In amending it, the assembly should show clearly what the committee or board is responsible for and what pertains to the entire organization. As a precaution, one could prefix to the report a statement such as this:

> **The report was adopted by the society after striking out what is enclosed in brackets and adding what is printed in footnotes.**

When a committee reports to the assembly on a resolution that was referred to it, the assembly's presiding officer should state the motion, depending on the recommendation of the committee, as follows:

- If the committee recommends that the resolution be adopted or makes no recommendation, the motion should be stated (by the chair) first on any pending amendment and then on the entire resolution: "The motion is on adopting the proposed amendment" *or* "The motion is on adopting the resolution."

- If the committee recommends that the resolution *not* be adopted, the motion nevertheless should be stated on adopting the resolution, perhaps adding: "the report of the committee to the contrary notwithstanding."

- If the committee recommends that the resolution be postponed indefinitely, or postponed to a certain time, the motion should be stated on postponing indefinitely or to a certain time.

- If the committee recommends that the resolution be amended in a certain way, the motion should be stated, first, on adopting the proposed amendment to the resolution and, then, on adopting the entire resolution.

In all of these cases, immediately after the committee's report is read, someone should make a motion as indicated above. The appropriate person to make it, if the committee makes any recommendation, is the committee member who reports to the assembly. If no one makes a motion, however, the assembly's chair should state the proper wording and ask if someone will make it. If someone has already made the proper motion, the chair should immediately state it (see Section 65).

A committee may submit a report that has a number of paragraphs or sections (such as a set of bylaws). In that case, the entire paper should be read by the member reporting or by the clerk, or secretary, of the assembly. Then the member reporting or someone else should move to adopt it unless this motion was already made.

After the assembly's chair has stated the motion on adopting the report, he or she should direct the member who reported or the assembly's clerk, or secretary, to read the first paragraph. *Paragraph* refers to a separate division of the proposition—for example, an article, a section, a paragraph, or a separate resolution.

No vote is taken on the adoption of each of the paragraphs; instead, upon completion, the entire paper is adopted. By not voting on the paragraphs one at a time, the assembly can go back after all have been amended and amend any of them further. In a committee, a similar paper would be treated the same way (see Section 28; see Section 48 for a practical example).

Should each paragraph be adopted separately, it would be improper afterward to vote on adopting the entire report. Similarly, it would be out of order to go back and amend a paragraph that was adopted until after it had been reconsidered.

After the first paragraph has been read to the assembly, the chair of the assembly should ask:

Are there any amendments proposed to this paragraph?

The chair should then pause for remarks or amendments, giving preference to the member who submitted the report if that person wants the floor. When satisfied that no one else wants the floor, the chair should state:

No (further) amendments being offered to this paragraph, the next will be read.

In this way, each paragraph is read and amended. Then the chair states that the entire report, or all of the resolutions, have been read and are open to *further* amendment. At this stage new paragraphs may be inserted, and even those originally in the report may be amended further since they have not yet been adopted. If there is a preamble, it should be read and amended after the body of the resolutions has been worded in final form. Then a vote is taken on adopting the entire report *as amended*.

When a committee reports back to an assembly on a paper (that was referred to it) with committee amendments, the reporting member reads only the amendments and then makes a motion to adopt them. The chair states the motion on the adoption of the amendments and asks for the first amendment to be read. After the reading, it's open to debate and further amendment by the assembly. A vote is then taken on adopting this amendment. After that, the next committee amendment is read and so on until all amendments are adopted or rejected. Only amendments to the committee's amendments are considered.

When the assembly is finished with the amendments, the chair of the assembly pauses for any further amendments to be proposed. When any such additional amendments are voted on, the chair puts to a vote the motion on agreeing to or adopting the entire paper as amended (except in a case such as revising the bylaws since they have already been adopted).

By suspending the rules (see Section 18) or by general consent, a report can be adopted immediately without following any of the above routine. (See Section 34 for the privileges in debate of the member making the report to the assembly.)

Section 32. Committee of the Whole

Sometimes an assembly wants to consider a subject and does not want to refer it to a committee. The subject may not be well understood, however, and may not be put into proper form for definite action. When, in such cases, the assembly wants to consider a subject with all of the freedom of an ordinary committee, the matter may be referred to a committee of the whole. The assembly then temporarily turns itself into such committee.

In large assemblies, such as the House of Representatives, where a member may speak only once on a question, a committee of the whole is a necessity. It allows the freest discussion of a subject, and yet at any time, the committee can "rise" (equivalent to adjourning in an assembly) and thus bring back into force the strict rules of the assembly.

When an assembly wants to consider a matter right away, and do so as a committee, someone should make a motion such as this:

> **I move that the assembly now resolve itself into a committee of the whole to consider _____.**

This is really a motion to Commit (see Section 22 for its order of precedence). If the motion passes, the presiding officer of the assembly immediately calls another member to take over the chair, and then the assembly's presiding officer temporarily takes his or her place as a member of the committee of the whole.

A committee of the whole operates under the rules of the assembly except as indicated in this section. The only motions in order are those to Amend, to adopt, and to "rise" and report, since a committee can't adjourn. Also, it can't order a vote by "yeas and nays" (see Section 38).

The only way to close or limit debate in a committee of the whole is for the assembly to vote that debate in the committee cease at a certain time or to vote that after a certain time no debate will be allowed except on new amendments. Even then, only one speech in favor of and one against, perhaps of five minutes each, should be allowed, or in some other way the time for debate should be regulated.

In Congress no motion to limit debate in a committee of the whole is in order until after the subject has already been considered in the committee. Since probably no subject would be considered more than once in a committee of the whole, the enforcement of this rule in an ordinary group would practically prevent such a group from putting any limit to debate in the committee.

If no limit to debate is prescribed, any member may speak as often as he or she can get the floor. The member also may speak each time as long as the time allowed for debate in the assembly, provided that no one wants the floor who has not spoken on the question. But if debate has been closed at a particular time by order of the assembly, the committee may not, even by unanimous consent, extend the time.

A committee of the whole may not refer a subject to another committee. Also, like other committees (see Section 28), it may not alter the text of any resolution referred to it. But if the resolution originates in the committee of the whole, all the associated amendments are incorporated in the resolution.

When a committee of the whole is through considering a subject referred to it or if it wants to adjourn or to have the regular assembly limit debate, someone should move that "the committee 'rise' and report," specifying the result of its proceedings. The motion to Rise in a committee, which is equivalent to the motion to Adjourn (Section 11) in an assembly, is always in order, except when another member has the floor, and it can't be debated.

As soon as the motion to Rise is adopted, the presiding officer returns to his or her place as chair of the regular assembly. The committee chair also returns to his or her place in the assembly, rises (in a large or formal meeting), and informs the presiding officer that:

The committee has gone through the business referred to it. I'm ready to make the report when the assembly is ready to receive it.

Or the committee chair may make such other report as is appropriate.

The assembly's clerk (or secretary) does not record the proceedings of the committee of the whole in the assembly's minutes but should keep a memo of the proceedings for the committee's use. In large meetings, the assembly's clerk vacates his or her seat so that it can be occupied by the chair of the committee. The assembly's assistant clerk then acts as clerk of the committee.

If a committee of the whole becomes disorderly and the committee chair is unable to maintain order, the assembly's presiding officer can take back the assembly chair and immediately declare the committee dissolved.

The quorum requirements for a committee of the whole is the same as that of the regular assembly (see Section 43). If the committee should find itself without a quorum, though, it would have to report that fact to the assembly. In that case, if there were no other business, the assembly would have to adjourn.

Section 33. Informal Consideration of a Question

Many assemblies, instead of converting to a committee of the whole, consider a matter informally; that is, they *act* as if they're in a committee of the whole. Then, afterward, they take formal action. In a small assembly, there's no objection to this.

According to U.S. Senate Rules 28 and 38, all Senate bills, joint resolutions, and treaties, upon a second reading, are considered "as if the Senate were in a committee of the whole," which is equivalent to considering a matter informally. But in large assemblies, it's better to follow the practice of the House and convert to a committee of the whole.

While acting informally on any resolutions, the assembly can only amend and adopt them. Without any further motion, the chair would then announce:

The assembly, acting informally [*or* "as in a committee of the whole"], has had _____ under consideration and has made certain amendments that will be reported.

The subject then comes before the assembly as if reported by a committee. While acting informally, the chair retains his or her assembly seat since it's not necessary to move that the committee "rise."

At any time, the informal consideration will end with the adoption of motions such as one to Adjourn (Section 11), to order the Previous Question (Section 20), and to Commit (Section 22) something to a committee, as well as any other motion except one to Amend (Section 23) something or to adopt a report. For example, the motion to Commit is equivalent to the following motions when an assembly is acting as a committee of the whole:

- That the committee "rise"

- That the committee of the whole be discharged from further consideration of the subject

- That a matter be referred to a committee

While an assembly is acting informally (as if in a committee of the whole), every member may speak as many times as desired and each time for as long as is allowed in the regular assembly (see Section 34). Also, the informal action may be rejected or altered by the assembly.

The assembly clerk should keep only a memo of the informal proceedings (not enter them in the assembly's minutes) since the information is only for temporary use. However, the chair's report to the assembly about the informal action should be entered in the minutes since it belongs to the assembly's regular proceedings.

Article V. Debate and Decorum

Section 34. Debate

When someone makes a motion and another member seconds it, the chair must state the motion to the assem-

bly before it's debated (read Sections 1–5 in connection
with this section on debate). A member who wants to
speak in debate should first rise (in a large or formal
meeting) and respectfully address the chair:

Mr. Chairman

Madam Chairman

The title *Mr. President* or *Madam President* is used when
that's the actual title of the presiding officer. *Mr.* or
Madam Moderator is common in religious meetings.
Brother Moderator is used in some parts of the country,
although it implies an equality between the speaker and
the chair that doesn't exist; only one is a moderator or
is in charge. Otherwise, a presiding officer should always
be addressed by his or her official title.

After being addressed, the chair will announce the member's
name (or show recognition in some other way). As
a matter of parliamentary courtesy (or rule in the case of
the U.S. House of Representatives), the member who has
made a motion bringing some subject before the assembly
is the one entitled to the floor first (see Section 2). This is
true even when someone else rises first and addresses the
chair. (With a committee report, the member who presents
the report is entitled to speak first). This person also is
entitled to close the debate but only after everyone who
wants to speak has had a chance to do so.

A member who reports a measure from a committee must
be given the right to close the debate. Therefore,
when someone calls for the Previous Question (Section
20), the chair immediately assigns the floor to the reporting
member to close the debate. Except for this
practice allowing someone to open and close the debate,
no one may speak more than twice on the same matter
and only once to a question of order (see Section 14).

Also, no one may speak more than ten minutes at a
time without permission from the assembly; the motion
requesting this permission must be decided by a two-thirds
vote (see Section 39) without debate. The time
limit for debate could vary, though, to suit the circumstances.
But a limit of two speeches of ten minutes each
is usually appropriate in ordinary groups. If greater free-

dom is needed, however, the assembly may refer the matter to a committee of the whole (see Section 32) or consider it informally (see Section 33). (On limiting or closing debate, see Section 37.)

In the House, no member may speak more than once on the same question or for more than one hour. The fourth rule of the Senate states: "No senator shall speak more than twice in any one debate, on the same day, without leave of the Senate, which question shall be decided without debate." If no such rule is adopted, each member can speak but once on the same matter.

No one may speak a second time on a question until every member who wants to speak has done so. Offering an amendment or making any other motion, however, changes the pending motion before the assembly to a different one. As far as debate is concerned, then, it is a new question.

Merely asking something or making a suggestion is not considered "speaking" on a question. Also, someone who makes a motion may *vote* against it but can't *speak* against the motion he or she made.

When an amendment is pending, the debate must be confined to the merits of that amendment. An exception to this rule would occur when the amendment is such that a decision on it practically decides the motion being amended.

The chair can't close the debate as long as anyone wants to speak. Even if a member claims the floor *after* the chair has put a motion to a vote or even after an affirmative vote has taken place—provided the negative has not been put to a vote—the member still has a right to resume the debate or make another motion.

Section 35. Undebatable Questions and Those That Open the Main Question to Debate

The following motions are decided without debate (all others are debatable):

- To Fix the Time to Which to Adjourn, when it's a privileged question (Section 10)

- To Adjourn or, in committee, to Rise (Section 11)

- To call for the Orders of the Day (Section 13) and questions about the priority of business

- To Appeal (Section 14), when made while a call for the Previous Question (Section 20) is pending or when simply relating to inappropriate behavior, transgressions of the rules about speaking, or the priority of business

- To Object to the Consideration of a Question (Section 15)

- To Lay [a matter] on the Table or to Take [it] from the Table (Section 19)

- To call for the Previous Question (Section 20)

- To Reconsider (Section 27) a motion that is itself undebatable

- Questions relating to the reading of papers (see Section 16), the withdrawal of a motion (see Section 17), suspending the rules (see Section 18), extending the limits of debate (see Section 34), limiting or closing debate (see Section 37), or granting permission to continue a speech to someone guilty of inappropriate behavior in debate (see Section 36)

The motion to Postpone [a matter] to a Certain Time (Section 21) allows only very limited debate that must focus on whether the postponement is appropriate. When an amendment is before an assembly, the question to be amended can't be debated unless it's necessarily involved in the amendment. But the following motions will open to discussion the entire merits of the main question:

- To Commit something to a committee (Section 22)

- To Postpone [a matter] Indefinitely (Section 24)

- To Rescind something (Section 25)

- To Reconsider a debatable question (Section 27)

It's important to keep in mind the distinction between debate and merely making suggestions or asking something. When asking something will help the assembly make a decision, it's allowed, to a limited extent, even though the motion before the group is undebatable.

Although free debate is allowed on every principal motion (see Section 6), it's either permitted or prohibited on other questions according to these principles:

- Usually, highly privileged questions shouldn't be debated. This is the case because they could be used to stop the assembly from voting on the main question. For example, if a motion to Adjourn (Section 11) were debatable, it could be used to hinder business. High privilege is generally not compatible with the right of debate on a privileged question.

- A motion that would suppress a matter before the assembly so that it couldn't be taken up during the current session (see Section 42) should have and does allow for free debate. A subsidiary motion (see Section 7), except one to Commit (see example below), is debatable only to the extent that the motion interferes with the right of the assembly to take up the original matter when desired.

English common parliamentary law makes all motions debatable unless some rule is adopted that limits debate. But every assembly is obliged to restrict debate on certain motions. The restrictions prescribed in Section 35 conform to the practice of Congress. There, however, it's very common to allow brief remarks on even the most undebatable questions, sometimes with five or six members speaking. This is permitted, though, only when no one objects.

The following examples point out the effect of various motions and hence the need for (or need to avoid) debate:

Example: To Postpone [a matter] Indefinitely (Section 24) prevents an assembly from taking it up again during that session. Therefore, free debate should be and is allowed for this motion, even involving the whole merits of the original question.

Example: To Postpone [a matter] to a Certain Time (Section 21) prevents an assembly from considering a question until the designated time. Therefore, this motion should have and does allow for limited debate on the appropriateness of the postponement.

Example: To Lay [a matter] on the Table (Section 19) means that the assembly can consider it at any time. Therefore, this motion need not be and isn't debatable. (See Section 19 concerning abuse of this motion.)

Example: To Commit (Section 22) a matter to a committee wouldn't be very debatable, according to the rule about opening the main question to debate. But it's an exception because it's often important for a committee to know the views of the assembly on a question. Thus it should be and is debatable, and it also opens to debate the entire matter to be referred to the committee.

Section 36. Decorum in Debate

In debate, you should confine yourself to the matter before the assembly and avoid personalities. You shouldn't reflect on any act of the assembly unless you intend to make a motion to Rescind (Section 25) the act while debating or at the conclusion of your remarks.

When you refer to another member, avoid using the person's name; instead, refer to the member as "the member who spoke last" or by some other impersonal designation. Always refer to the officers of the assembly by their official titles (see Section 2).

Although you shouldn't question the motives of a member, you may strongly condemn the nature or consequences of some measure proposed by that member. In other words, it's not the person but the measure that should be the subject of debate.

When the chair rises to state a point of order, give information, or say something else, within the limits of the chair's authority (see Section 40), the person speaking must sit down until the chair is heard first.

When someone is called to order, that person must sit down until the question of order is decided. If the member's remarks are decided to be improper, that person may not continue speaking if anyone objects unless he or she gets the permission of the assembly (by majority vote); no debate is allowed on that question.

Disorderly words should be written down by the person who objects to them or by the clerk (or secretary) of the assembly and then read to the member. If the member denies having said them, the assembly will have to decide (by majority vote) whether or not they really are the member's words. If a member can't justify the words he or she used but won't apologize for using them, the assembly may take action.

If the disorderly words are personal, involving another member, the two persons should leave the room. (Usually, a person should not be present when an assembly is debating something about that person.) Then the assembly can proceed to consider the case. The person who objected to the words, however, doesn't have to leave unless he or she is one of the parties involved in the case. But if any business has taken place since the member spoke, it's too late to act on the disorderly words.

During debate and while the chair is speaking or the assembly is engaged in voting, no one is allowed to disturb the assembly by whispering or walking around or doing anything else that might be distracting or disruptive.

Section 37. Closing Debate

Debate on a motion is *not* closed by the chair rising to put the question to a vote. Until *both* the affirmative and negative have been voted on, a member can claim the floor and reopen debate (see Section 38). However, debate can be closed by making the motions listed below. The first two close debate only by suppressing the question itself. (For the circumstances under which each of the motions can be used to suppress debate or suppress other motions, see Section 58 and 59.)

The motions given below can't be debated and, except for the motion to Lay [a matter] on the Table (Section 19), require a two-thirds vote to be adopted.

- An Objection to the Consideration of a Question (Section 15) is allowed only when the motion to which someone objects is first made. If the objection is sustained, it not only stops the debate on the objectionable motion but also throws the subject out of the assembly for the current session (see Section 42). This is the effect for which it was designed.

- The motion to Lay [a matter] on the Table (Section 19), if adopted, carries the pending motion to the table. For the tabled motion to be taken from the table, there must be a majority vote.

- A call for the Previous Question (Section 20), if adopted, cuts off debate on a subject and brings the assembly to a vote on the matter being discussed. An exception would be when the pending motion is a motion to Amend (Section 23) something or to Commit (Section 22) it to a committee. In that case, the vote is taken not only on the motion to Amend or Commit but also on the question to be amended or committed—unless someone demands that a vote be taken only on the motion to Amend or to Commit. When the Previous Question is ordered only on an amendment, or an amendment of an amendment (see Section 23), debate is closed and a vote is taken immediately on the amendment. The effect of the Previous Question is then exhausted (no longer exists), and new amendments can be offered and debated.

- An assembly can adopt an order to *limit debate* on a special subject in regard to the number or length of speeches. It can also decide to *close debate* on the subject at a stated time, and all pending questions must then be put to a vote without further debate. Either measure may be applied simply to a pending amendment or to an amendment of an amendment. When this is voted on, the original question is still open to debate and amendment.

In the House, where each member may speak for an hour, any of the motions to cut off debate can be adopted by a mere majority. In practice, however, they are not used until after some debate. Rule 28 of the House provides that forty minutes, twenty on each side, are allowed for debate whenever the Previous Question (Section 20) is ordered on a proposition for which there has been no debate or when the rules are suspended (see Section 18). In ordinary groups, harmony is so essential that a two-thirds vote should be required to force the group to a final vote without allowing free debate (see Section 39).

Article VI. Vote

Section 38. Voting

When it's not allowed to modify or debate a motion, the chair should immediately put the motion to a vote. With a debatable matter, however, the chair should wait until it appears that the debate has ended and then ask if the assembly is ready for the question (ready to vote). If no one rises or speaks, the chair can put the matter to a vote.

Different parts of the country use different forms for putting a motion to a vote. The U.S. House of Representatives uses this form:

As many as are in favor [*as the question may be*] say aye.

After the ayes are said, the next question is:

As many as are opposed say no.

The following form is more common in ordinary groups:

It has been moved and seconded that _____.
Those in favor of the motion say aye. [*Pause*
for the yes vote]. **Those opposed say no.**

A show of hands is also used in ordinary groups. For example, suppose that a motion has been made to adopt a certain resolution. After it has been read, the chair might state:

You've heard the resolution read. Those in
favor of its adoption raise their right hands.
[*Pause for the yes vote.*] **Those opposed do**
the same.

These examples show two methods of putting a motion to a vote, with the affirmative vote taken first. (See Section 65; see also Forms of Putting Certain Questions in the Quick-Reference Guide to Motions.)

A majority of the votes actually cast is sufficient to adopt any motion that's in order except those mentioned in Section 39; they require a two-thirds vote. A plurality vote never adopts a motion or elects anyone to office unless a special rule allowing it was adopted previously (see Section 39).

When a vote is taken, the chair should announce the results, for example:

The motion is carried—the resolution is adopted.

The ayes have it—the resolution is adopted.

When the chair announces a vote, if anyone then rises and states that he or she doubts the vote or calls for a "division" of the motion, the chair should put it to a vote:

A division is called for; those in favor of the
motion please rise.

After counting them and announcing the number, the chair would continue:

Those opposed please rise.

The chair would next count the no votes, announce the number, and state whether the motion is carried or lost.

The chair could also direct the secretary or appoint tellers to make the count and report the numbers to him or her. When tellers are appointed, they should be selected from both sides of a question—for and against. When a vote is not taken by ballot, members may change their votes but only *before* a decision on the question has been finally and conclusively pronounced by the chair.

Until the negative position has been put to a vote, any member may rise and speak, make motions for amendment or otherwise, and thus renew the debate just as if voting had never started. This is true whether or not the member was in the room when an affirmative version of the motion was put to a vote. When a member rises to speak before the "no" votes are requested, therefore, the motion is considered to be in the same state as if it had never been put to a vote.

A member can't vote on a motion that affects him or her personally, such as when the person is named in a resolution. But if more than one name is included in the resolution, all are entitled to vote. (A sense of propriety would stop most people from exercising this right unless their vote was necessary to change the outcome.)

Otherwise, a minority could control an assembly simply by including the names of a sufficient number of persons in a motion. This might occur, for example, with motions bringing charges against certain persons or even suspending or expelling them from the assembly. (After charges are preferred against a member and the assembly has ordered the person to appear for trial, the member is theoretically "under arrest," or restrained, and is deprived of all rights of membership until his or her case is disposed of. See Section 69.)

A motion fails if there's a tie vote unless the presiding officer, exercising the right of the chair to cast a deciding vote, votes yes. If the chair's vote would cause a tie, however, the chair could cast a negative vote to defeat a measure.

When an Appeal (Section 14) is made concerning a

decision the chair makes, he or she should ask for a vote on the matter:

Shall the decision of the chair stand as the judgment of the assembly?

Shall the decision of the chair be sustained?

A tie vote would uphold the chair's decision because a group can reverse a chair's decision only by majority vote. Therefore, a tie vote (no majority) wouldn't be sufficient to reverse it, and that in effect would mean that the chair's decision would stand.

An assembly can also vote by ballot. This method of voting is used when a group's charter, articles of incorporation, or constitution or its bylaws require it or when the assembly has ordered that a vote be taken by ballot. To vote by ballot, the chair would appoint at least two tellers. They would distribute slips of paper on which the members, including the chair, would write their vote. If the chair should forget to vote when everyone else does, before the ballots are counted, he or she must *get* the permission of the assembly to vote afterward.

In voting for candidates in ordinary groups, the ballots may have incorrectly written names; nevertheless, they should be counted as a vote for the intended candidate whenever that intention is clear. In voting by ballot, members also may vote for persons who weren't nominated. Although closing nominations means that other candidates can't be endorsed publicly, it doesn't stop members from voting for and electing them.

After the votes are collected, they're counted by the tellers. In counting the ballots, all blanks are ignored. The result is then reported to the chair, who announces it to the assembly. In the case of an election to office, the chair might state:

The whole number of votes cast is _____; the number necessary for election is _____. Mr. Castell received _____; Ms. Williams, _____; Mrs. Reuben, _____. Mr. Castell, having received the required number, is elected _____.

When there's only one candidate for office and the organization's charter, articles of incorporation, or constitution requires a vote by ballot, an assembly may authorize the secretary, or clerk, to cast the vote of the assembly for the one candidate. (If anyone objects, though, ballots must be handled in the usual way.) This can be done only by unanimous consent, however, and it's doubtful that it should even be allowed. But if a motion is made to make a vote unanimous and someone objects, the motion fails. An election, like other matters voted on, takes effect immediately unless there's a rule to the contrary.

By majority vote, an assembly can order that the vote on any question be taken by "yeas and nays." Voting by yeas and nays, a method peculiar to the United States, has the effect of placing on the record how each member votes. But it takes a great deal of time and is rarely used by ordinary groups.

Under the U.S. Constitution, in both the House and the Senate, one-fifth of the members present can order a vote to be taken by yeas and nays. To avoid some of the resulting inconveniences, Congress has required, for instance, that the call for the Previous Question must be seconded by a majority. That step avoids taking the yeas and nays until a majority are in favor of ordering that the main question come to a vote. This method of voting is very useful in representative bodies, especially when the proceedings are published. It lets the people know how their representatives voted on important measures. In an ordinary group, if there's not a legal or constitutional provision for a minority ordering the yeas and nays, the organization should adopt a rule allowing the yeas and nays to be ordered by one-fifth vote, as occurs in Congress, or even a much smaller number. In some small groups, a single member can demand that a vote on a resolution be taken by the yeas and nays.

To vote by yeas and nays, the chair must state both sides

of a matter at once. The secretary, or clerk, then calls the roll, and as each member's name is called, that person rises (in a formal setting) and answers yes (or aye) or no.

After the roll call, the secretary would read the names of those who voted yes, followed by those who voted no. Any mistakes in the record are corrected before the secretary gives the number voting on each side to the chair, who will then announce the result. With a vote by yeas and nays, an entry must be made in the minutes of all persons voting yes and all voting no.

The chair may use a form similar to the following in putting a question to a vote by yeas and nays:

> **As many as are in favor of the adoption of these resolutions will, when their names are called, answer yes [*or* "aye"]; those opposed will answer no.**

> **Those in favor of adopting these resolutions will answer yes [*or* "aye"] when their names are called. Those opposed will answer no.**

The chair then directs the secretary to call the roll. Since both the affirmative and negative are put to a vote at the same time, as shown in the above examples, it's too late for anyone to renew debate after one person has answered the roll call. Also, once the roll call begins, it's too late for anyone to ask to be excused from voting.

Voting by yeas and nays can never be used to hinder business as long as the above rule is observed. But it shouldn't be used at all in a mass meeting or in any other assembly where the members are not responsible to a constituency. Also, the yeas and nays can't be ordered in a committee of the whole (see Section 32).

Section 39. Motions Requiring More Than a Majority Vote

A *majority* vote means a majority of the votes actually cast, just as a two-thirds vote refers to two-thirds of the votes actually cast. Blanks are never counted. Sometimes the bylaws of an organization provide for a vote of two-thirds of the members *present* or two-thirds of the *total membership,* both of which are very different requirements from one specifying two-thirds of the *votes cast.*

> *Example:* **Suppose that twelve members vote on a matter in a meeting where twenty are present and the total membership is thirty. A two-thirds vote (of those voting) would be eight; a two-thirds vote of those present would be fourteen; a two-thirds vote of the entire membership would be twenty. In this case, a majority vote (of those voting) would be seven.**

A *plurality* vote occurs when someone has more votes for a certain office or position than any of the rivals. In civil government, as a rule all officers elected by a popular vote are elected by a plurality. But in a deliberative assembly, where voting may be repeated until someone is elected, a plurality never elects unless there's a special rule allowing it.

The following motions require a two-thirds vote to be adopted since a mere majority shouldn't be able to deprive others of the right to discuss something and the right to have the rules enforced. Motions other than those listed below, however, require only a majority:

- To Amend the Rules (Section 45; also requires previous notice)

- To Suspend the Rules (Section 18)

- To make a Special Order (Sections 13, 61)

- To Take Up a Question Out of Its Proper Order (Section 13)

- To Object to Consideration of a Question (Section 15; a negative vote on considering a matter must be two-thirds to discuss the matter for the current session)

- To Extend the Limits of Debate (Section 34)

- To Limit or Close Debate (Section 37)

- To call for the Previous Question (Section 20)

Every motion in the preceding list suspends or changes some rule or custom of a deliberative body. The first two, by their title, obviously have the effect of changing a rule or custom. But the others have a similar effect, even though their title may not immediately suggest this.

> *Example:* To make a Special Order suspends all of the rules that interfere with the consideration of a question at the specified time.

> *Example:* To Take Up a Question Out of Its Proper Order is a change in the order of business.

> *Example:* An Objection to the Consideration of a Question, if the motion passes, suspends or conflicts with the right of a member to introduce a measure in the assembly. That right has been established by a custom and seems to be essential to the very idea of a deliberative body.

> *Example:* To Extend the Limits of Debate is to suspend a rule or order of an assembly.

> *Example:* The call for the Previous Question and motions to Close or Limit Debate force an assembly to take final action on a matter without allowing further or any discussion. In other words, they suspend the fundamental principle of deliberative bodies that an assembly won't be forced to take final action on a matter until everyone has had a chance to discuss its merits. (Although a majority can stop debate by tabling a question, the assembly can take it from the table at any time. A majority of members, however, can still use this means to get rid of a matter at least until they're ready to consider it.)

In spite of the need for members to be able to discuss motions, there are times when it's useful to suspend the right to introduce and debate matters just as it might be advantageous to suspend the rules of an assembly or change the order of business. Nevertheless, if a bare majority could suspend or change rules and privileges, those rules and privileges wouldn't be of much value. Experience has shown that a two-thirds vote should be required to adopt any motion that could suspend or change the rules or established order of business, and the rule requiring a two-thirds vote on the motions listed previously is based on this general principle.

Old parliamentary practice required unanimous consent to suspend the rules. The House requires only a majority to call for the Previous Question, to Close or Limit Debate, and to sustain an Objection to the Consideration of a Question (a rule no longer taken advantage of). Because of the huge amount of business to be transacted and the larger number of members in the House, each entitled to speak in debate for an hour, it's necessary for them to allow a majority to Limit or Close Debate. This is especially significant in Congress, since the minority party could practically stop legislation if it could also prevent debate from being cut off. Groups that have partisan members should, like Congress, allow a bare majority to call for the Previous Question and to Limit or Close Debate. (See Section 38 in regard to ordering the yeas and nays by a one-fifth vote in Congress; see also the discussion of congressional procedure in the Introduction.)

Article VII. The Officers and the Minutes

Section 40. Chairman or President

When no special title has been assigned, the presiding officer is usually called the chair or chairman (in religious assemblies, the moderator). The assembly's charter, articles of incorporation, or constitution may prescribe a title such as president. (See Section 34; also read Sections 2, 24, 44, and 65 in connection with this section.)

The presiding officer's duties are as follows:

- To open the session at the required time by taking the chair and calling the meeting to order

- To announce business before the assembly in the order it must be acted on (see Section 44)

- To state and put to a vote (see Sections 38 and 65) all motions that are made regularly and those that arise during the meeting

- To announce the result of a vote on motions

- To restrain members engaged in debate within the rules of order (when the disorder is so great that business can't be transacted and the chair can't enforce order, to adjourn the assembly as a last resort)

- To enforce order and proper conduct (see Section 36) on all occasions among the members

- To decide all Questions of Order (subject to an Appeal [Section 14] to the assembly by any two members)

- To inform the assembly about a point of order or practice when necessary or when called on to do so

- To authenticate by his or her signature, when necessary, all of the acts, orders, and proceedings of the assembly

- To represent and stand for the assembly in general, declaring its will and always obeying its rules

In a formal setting, the chair rises (stands up) to put a motion to a vote but in an informal setting may remain seated. (In very small groups, though, such as a committee or board of trustees, the chair wouldn't stand up.) Formally, the presiding officer also rises (without calling anyone forward) when speaking on a Question of Order (the chair is entitled to speak before other members when he or she chooses to do so).

The chair always refers to himself or herself as "the chair," not "I":

> **The chair has decided that . . . [*not* "I have decided that . . ."]**

When a member has the floor, the chair can't interrupt as long as the member doesn't break any rules of the assembly (except as described in Section 2).

The chair may vote when voting is done by ballot and in all other cases when the vote would change the result. (But the chair must vote *before* the tellers have started to count the ballets; otherwise, the permission of the assembly is needed.)

> *Example:* **Suppose that a two-thirds vote is needed to pass a motion and the chair's vote with the minority would cause the motion to fail. In that case the chair is entitled to vote since doing so would change the result. In the same way, the chair may vote with the minority if doing so would create a tie vote. That would also cause the motion to fail, since it must have a majority or two-thirds vote depending on the specific motion and the applicable requirement.**

If someone makes a motion that refers to the chair, the presiding officer shouldn't put the question to a vote. Instead, the secretary must put it to a vote, or if the secretary doesn't do it, the person making the motion may do so.

If the presiding officer has to leave, he or she may appoint a chairman pro tem. But the first adjournment puts an end to that appointment, and the assembly can end it earlier by electing another chair. When there are vice-presidents, however, the first one on the list who is present acts as chair in the absence of the regular presiding officer and should always be called to the chair in such cases.

The regular chair, knowing that he or she will be absent from a future meeting, nevertheless may not authorize another member to fill in. In such a case—when there are no vice-presidents—the secretary, or clerk (see Section 4), or, in that person's absence, any other member at this future meeting should call the meeting to order and see to it that a chairman pro tem is elected.

The chairman pro tem who is elected would then hold office during that session (see Section 42) unless or until the regular chair returned. Again, the exception would be that if there were vice-presidents in the meeting, instead of a chairman pro tem being elected, the first vice-president would be called to assume the chair.

The presiding officer sometimes calls a member to take over the chair so that he or she can take part in the debate. As a rule, though, this shouldn't be done. Moreover, it never should be done when the members clearly object to it or when there might be difficulty in preserving order because of it. Whenever a chair gives the appearance of being partisan, he or she loses much of the ability to control the opposition. (See Section 28 for the duties of committee chairs.)

Many presiding officers have a bad habit of speaking on matters before the assembly, even interrupting a member who has the floor. This is unjustified in both common parliamentary law and in the practice of Congress. Someone who wants or expects to take an active part in debate shouldn't accept the position of chair.

> It is a general rule in all deliberative assemblies that the presiding officer shall not participate in the debate, or other proceedings, in any other capacity than as such officer. He is only allowed, therefore, to state matters of fact within his knowledge; to inform the assembly on points of order or the course of proceeding, when called upon for that purpose, or when he finds it necessary to do so; and, on appeals from his decision on questions of order, to address the assembly in debate. (Cushing's Manual, Section 202)

> Though the speak [chair] may of right speak to matters of order and be first heard, he is restrained from speaking on any other subject except where the assembly have occasion for

facts within his knowledge; then he may, with their leave, state the matter of fact. (Jefferson's Manual, Section xvii; and Barclay's "Digest of the Rules and Practice of the House of Representatives U.S.," page 195)

The chair must be familiar with parliamentary usage and set an example of conforming strictly to it. But no rules will take the place of tact and common sense. A chair usually wouldn't wait for someone to make routine motions or for a motion to be seconded when it's clearly favored by others (see Section 65). But if others object to proceeding in that manner, it's safer to insist instantly that the forms of parliamentary law be observed.

Many things can be done by general consent to save time, but when an assembly is large or divided, and when some members are continually raising points of order, the best course is to enforce strictly all of the rules and forms of parliamentary law.

When an improper motion is made, the chair shouldn't simply rule it out of order. Instead, the chair should suggest a better way to accomplish whatever is intended:

Example: Suppose that someone moves to postpone a matter. The chair should explain that if the time isn't specified, the proper motion is for the question to Lay on the Table (Section 19).

Example: Suppose that someone moves to table something until a certain time. The chair should suggest that the proper motion is to Postpone [the matter] to a Certain Time (Section 21).

Example: Suppose that someone moves to reject a resolution. The chair should state that the proper motion is to Postpone [the resolution] Indefinitely (Section 24).

A chair also should have executive ability and be capable of controlling people. But to control others, one has to control one's self. An excited chair will likely cause trouble in a meeting. (For hints to inexperienced chairs, see Section 50.)

A chair shouldn't let the purpose of a meeting be defeated by people who are using parliamentary forms to obstruct business. In such a case, the chair should refuse to entertain a motion that causes delay.

If an appeal is made by the opposition, the chair must entertain it. But if the chair's decision is sustained by a large majority, he or she can then refuse to entertain any further appeal made by the opposing faction while it's continuing its obstruction. The chair shouldn't, however, adopt such a course merely to expedite business when the opposition isn't trying to obstruct the proceedings.

Sometimes a presiding officer is perplexed with the difficulties that go with the position of chair. In such cases, it's best to heed the advice of a writer on parliamentary law who once said:

> The great purpose of all rules and forms is to subserve the will of the assembly rather than to restrain it; to facilitate, and not to obstruct, the expression of their deliberate sense.

Section 41. Clerk, or Secretary, and the Minutes

The officer who records the proceedings of a meeting is usually called the *clerk* or *secretary,* and the record of the meeting is called the *minutes*. When there are two secretaries, the one who records the meeting activity is called the recording secretary. The other one is called the corresponding secretary.

In many organizations, the secretary not only acts as recording officer but also collects the dues of members. To that extent, the secretary is also a financial officer. When the treasurer acts as banker, paying bills only on the order of the organization, signed by the secretary alone or by the president and secretary, the secretary becomes the financial officer and should report to the organization on income received and its source, as well as money spent and why. (See Section 52 for the secretary's duties as financial officer.)

The secretary's desk should be near that of the chair. If the chair is absent and there is no vice-president attending the meeting, the secretary should call the meeting to order when the time arrives. The secretary would then preside until the assembly elects a chairman pro tem, which should be done immediately.

The secretary should keep a record of the proceedings (see Section 51), which might begin like this:

> **At a regular quarterly meeting of [*organization*], held on the 31st day of March 19XX, at [*place*], with [*name of president or chair*] presiding, the minutes were read by the secretary and approved.**

If the regular secretary had been absent, the wording might be as follows:

> **A regular quarterly meeting of [*organization*] was held on the 31st day of March 19XX, at [*place*], with [*name of president or chair*] presiding. The secretary being absent, [*name*] was appointed secretary pro tem. The minutes were then read and approved.**

If the minutes were not read, the statement about the minutes should be changed to something like this:

> **The reading of the minutes was dispensed with.**

Essential points to make in the opening paragraph of the minutes included the following:

- The kind of meeting: regular (quarterly, biannual, or the like) or special; or adjourned regular or adjourned special
- The name of the assembly

- The date and place of the meeting (place can be omitted if it is always the same)

- The fact of the presence of the regular chair and secretary or, in their absence, the names of their substitutes

- Whether or not the minutes of the previous meeting were read and approved or whether the reading was dispensed with

The person responsible for taking the minutes should write neatly, leaving room for corrections. (Depending on the organization and the type of meeting, notes may be taken manually or by machine. Machine recordings, however, should always be backed up by notes.) The notes would be transferred to a permanent minute book or file, and the minutes would then be taken to the next meeting of the organization to be read for corrections and approval.

The secretary may keep the original notes taken during the meeting in a pocket memo book that can be carried to every meeting. These original notes, as corrected, are approved and then transferred into the permanent record. The original notes should always be kept until they're compared carefully with the permanent record.

After an assembly approves the minutes, without a reconsideration, it may correct them further at any future time no matter how much time has elapsed or how many times they have already been amended. The official version of the minutes (not the original notes) must be signed by the person who acted as secretary for that meeting. In some organizations, the chair must also sign them. When they're published, both officers should sign them. (See also the description of taking and preparing minutes in Chapter 8 in the first part of the book on meeting arrangements).

In deciding how to keep the minutes, a lot depends on the kind of meeting and whether the minutes will be published. Regardless, the secretary must never use the minutes personally to commend or criticize something said or done in a meeting.

If the minutes are going to be published, it's often far more interesting to know what leading speakers said rather than what resolutions were adopted or what routine business was transacted. In such cases, when details are extensive, the secretary may need at least one assistant to help prepare the minutes for publication.

In meetings of ordinary groups or boards, there is no point in reporting debates. The secretary in such cases primarily records what is done, not what is said. Unless some rule states otherwise, the secretary should enter every principal motion (see Section 6) that comes before the assembly, whether it's adopted or rejected.

When there's a division of a motion (see Section 38) or when the vote is by ballot, the secretary should enter the number of votes on each side. When the voting is by "yeas and nays" (see Section 38), the secretary should enter a list of the names of those voting on each side.

The secretary should note on committee reports the date they were received, state what further action was taken on them, and preserve them among the various records that are the secretary's responsibility.

In the minutes, the secretary should summarize any report that was agreed to unless the report contains resolutions. In that case, the resolutions should be entered in full as adopted by the assembly but not as though it were the report that was accepted.

With a particularly important report, the assembly should order it "to be entered in the minutes." The secretary would then include the full report. But the proceedings of a committee of the whole (see Section 32) or while the assembly is acting informally (see Section 33) should *not* be entered in the regular assembly's minutes.

Before an adjournment "without day [*sine die*]," when it will be a long time until the next meeting, the secretary usually reads the current minutes for approval, rather than wait until the next meeting. But if the next meeting will be held within a reasonable time, the secretary should wait and read them at the next meeting. They would be adopted then (after being corrected, if necessary).

If errors in the minutes are discovered later, they must

be corrected again, no matter how much time has elapsed or how many times previously they were corrected. The corrections are handled, without making a motion to Reconsider them, by a simple vote to amend the minutes.

The secretary has custody of the minutes and all other official documents that come before an assembly. Every member, however, has the right to inspect the minutes, and the chair can even order that certain minutes must be turned over to a committee that needs them to perform its duties.

Before each meeting, the secretary should prepare an order of business (see Section 44) for the chair to use. This would show everything expected to come before the assembly, each item in its exact order. The secretary also should bring to each meeting a list of all standing committees and any existing select committees. When another committee is appointed, the secretary should hand to the committee chair or some other committee member(s) the names of the committee members and all papers referred to the committee.

Article VIII. Miscellaneous

Section 42. Session

A *session* of an assembly is a meeting, or a number of adjourned (continued) meetings, that may last several days (e.g., a session of a convention) or several months (e.g., a session of Congress) but altogether is considered *one* unit. The term *meeting* refers to an assembling together of members of a group for any length of time, with no separation by adjournment.

An adjournment to meet later, even the same day, ends a meeting but *not* a session, since the session includes all of the adjourned meetings. The *next* meeting, then, would be an "adjourned meeting" in the *same* session.

A meeting ends by temporary adjournment; a session, which may consist of many meetings, ends by adjournment "without day." A *recess* is a pause or break in the proceedings taken for perhaps a few minutes. But it doesn't end a meeting. The intermediate adjournments from day to day or the recesses taken during the day, therefore, don't destroy the continuity of a meeting—in reality, together they make up one session.

Any meeting that is *not* an adjournment of another meeting begins a new session. In a permanent organization that has regular meetings every week, month, or year, for example, each individual meeting constitutes a separate session of the organization. That session, however, can be prolonged by adjourning a meeting to another day.

Under ordinary circumstances, you can end a meeting simply by moving to Adjourn (Section 11). The group may meet again at the time specified by the organization's rules or by a resolution that sets the time.

If the group doesn't meet until the time specified in the bylaws for the next regular meeting, an adjournment is said to close the session and, in effect, is an adjournment "without day." But if the group had previously set a time for the next meeting by vote or by adopting a program that covers several meetings (or days), the adjournment is, in effect, "to a certain day." It, therefore, does *not* close the session. When an assembly has meetings several days in a row, they all constitute one session.

If a principal motion (see Section 6) is postponed indefinitely (see Section 24) or rejected in one session, it can't be introduced again at that particular session (see Section 26). But it can be introduced at the next session as long as a rule of the assembly doesn't prohibit it. So a matter that was tabled (see Section 19) at one session can be introduced as a new motion at any succeeding session. The only way to introduce that matter at the same session would be to move to Take it from the Table (Section 19).

No session may interfere with the assembly's rights at any future session unless the charter, articles of incorporation, or constitution or its bylaws or rules of order allow it. Such documents aren't changed suddenly—they require notice of any proposed amendment and then at least a two-thirds vote for adoption—rather, they're considered an expression of the deliberative views (and possibly the legal requirements) of an entire organization, not merely the opinions or wishes of any particular meeting.

> *Example:* If a presiding officer were temporarily ill, an assembly couldn't elect another chair to hold office for longer than the current session. By following the prescribed steps for an *election* to fill a vacancy, however, giving whatever notice is necessary, an assembly could legally elect a chair to hold office as long as the regular chair was absent.

Although one session of an assembly can't control or dictate to the next session of the assembly, any session may adopt a permanent rule or resolution that continues in force until it's rescinded (see Section 49). Nevertheless, such standing rules won't interfere with future sessions since a majority can suspend or rescind them (see Section 25) or adopt new standing rules at any moment. Therefore, it's pointless for an assembly to postpone something to a day beyond the next succeeding session in an attempt to stop the next session from considering a question. On the other hand, one may not move to Reconsider (Section 27) a vote taken at a previous session. But the motion to Reconsider can be called up if it was made at the last *meeting* of the previous session (see Section 60). Also, committees may be appointed to report at a future session.

In all legislative bodies, including Congress, the limits of a session are clearly defined. In ordinary groups, however, with more or less frequent meetings, this matter causes a lot of confusion. Any organization may decide what constitutes a session. But if there's no rule clarifying this, common parliamentary law would make each regular or special meeting a *separate* session.

There are significant disadvantages to a rule that makes a session include all of the meetings of an ordinary group over a long period, such as a year (see Sections 24 and 26). The members of an organization also might take advantage of the freedom that comes from considering each regular meeting a separate session and might repeatedly renew unprofitable motions.

In the latter case, the group could adopt a rule prohibiting the second introduction of any principal motion (see Section 6) within, say, three or six months after its rejection, after indefinite postponement, or after the group refused to consider it. Generally, though, it's better to suppress the undesirable motion simply by making another motion refusing to consider it (see Section 15).

Section 43. Quorum

A *quorum* is the number needed in a meeting to transact business. Unless there's a special rule to the contrary, the quorum of every assembly is a majority of all members. A permanent organization, however, usually adopts a smaller number as a quorum, even less than one-twentieth of the members. A small number for a quorum is necessary in large groups because only a small percentage of the members are ever present at a meeting.

Although a quorum may transact any business, it's usually best not to transact important business unless the meeting has a fair attendance (more than a quorum) or unless previous notice of the proposed action was given. To act by unanimous consent, at least a quorum has to be present.

In the English Parliament, the House of Lords (about four hundred and fifty members) can transact business if only three members are present. The House of Commons (about six hundred and seventy members) requires only forty members for a quorum. But the U.S. Constitution (Article 1, Section 5) states that a majority of each house of Congress is needed for a quorum to do business.

The presiding officer at a meeting shouldn't take the chair until a quorum is present, unless there's no hope of a quorum attending. Then no business can be transacted except moving to Adjourn (Section 11). If no one objects, though, debate may continue, but the only vote that may be taken is the one for adjournment.

In a committee of the whole, the quorum requirement is the same as for the regular assembly. In any other committee, a majority is required unless the assembly orders otherwise. Also, a committee has to wait for a quorum before proceeding to undertake its business. If later in a meeting the number falls below quorum requirements, business isn't interrupted unless a member points it out. Nevertheless, no matter can be decided (voted on) unless a quorum is present.

Boards of trustees, managers, directors, and so on usually have the same quorum requirement as a committee—a majority of the members. The organization that appoints a board delegates its power to the board and decides what number is needed for it to transact business. Therefore, the organization could decide on a number other than a majority. But if it doesn't specify another number, the requirement is considered to be a majority.

It's important to be careful in amending the rule about a quorum. An assembly might want to change the quorum requirement from one number to another. If it acts first to strike out the old number without specifying the new number at the same time, the quorum requirement instantly becomes a majority. The problem is that it then may not ever be possible to get a majority together to make the desired change. Without a majority present, there won't be a quorum to transact business and adopt the new rule specifying a different number for a quorum.

The proper procedure, instead, to amend a rule about the quorum, is to strike out certain words (or the whole rule) *and* insert certain other words (or the new rule)—all at the same time. In that way, the matter will be voted on as one question.

Section 44. Order of Business

Every permanent organization must adopt an order of business (the order in which things will be considered) for its meetings. When an organization doesn't do this, the following order should be observed:

- Reading of the minutes of the previous meeting (if several meetings a day are held, it's sufficient to read the minutes just once, usually at the first meeting of the day)

- Reports of standing committees (boards of directors, trustees, and so on are in this category)

- Reports of select committees

- Unfinished business (Orders of the Day [Section 13], which includes business postponed to the current meeting, is in this category)

- New business

If a subject has been made a Special Order (Section 13) for the day, it has precedence over all other business except the reading of the minutes.

If you want to transact business out of the specified order, it's necessary to move to Suspend the Rules (Section 18); that requires a two-thirds vote. Or as each resolution or report comes up, a majority can immediately table it (see Section 19). They can thereby keep moving things out of the way until reaching the matter they want to consider first.

It's improper, though, to table or postpone an entire class of questions (such as committee reports). In fact, it's improper to put aside anything except the matter currently before the assembly (see Section 19).

Section 45. Amendments of Rules of Order

Rules of order may be amended at any regular meeting of an assembly by two-thirds vote provided that the amendment was submitted *in writing* at the previous regular meeting. At least equal notice and a two-thirds vote are needed to amend the charter, articles of incorporation, or constitution or the bylaws of an organization (subject to any state laws or legal requirements).

These documents and the rules of order should contain a provision that they can't be amended by less than a two-thirds vote and not without previous notice of the proposed amendment. The notice is meant to let the members know what the amendment is and that it's going to be considered and acted on at a certain time.

Notice isn't required, however, to amend the original amendment. If that were the case, it would be virtually impossible to amend the charter, articles of incorporation, or constitution or the bylaws and rules of order.

The amendment to the original amendment has to be relevant to that original amendment. Also, no other amendment is in order or may delay action on the original amendment.

Often an organization's bylaws state that an amendment has to be read at a certain number of regular meetings before it can be acted on; the first reading is by the secretary, or clerk, when it's proposed. After the last reading, it's up for action. If an amendment has to be read at three regular meetings, for instance, in an organization that holds regular weekly meetings, action on it would be delayed until two weeks after it was first proposed.

Part II.
Organization and
Conduct of Business

Article IX. Organization and Meetings

Section 46. Occasional or Mass Meeting

Organization. Not all meetings are held by members of an organized group. When no organized group is involved, and various persons simply meet to conduct business, someone (anyone) in the group should start the meeting by stepping forward and stating:

> **The meeting will please come to order. I move that [*name of someone present*] act as chair of this meeting.**

Someone else should reply:

> **I second the motion.**

The person making the motion then puts the motion to a vote:

> **It has been moved and seconded that [*name*] act as chair of this meeting. Those in favor say aye. [*Pause for the affirmative vote.*] Those opposed say no.**

If the majority votes in favor, the person who started the meeting states:

> **The motion is carried. [*Name*] will take the chair.**

If the motion fails, however, he or she will announce

that fact and ask that someone else be nominated. The above process is then repeated. (The dialogue in this section is a suggested wording for people in ordinary meetings. Although it's a common and proper form, the exact wording may vary.)

Sometimes a member of a group nominates a chair and no vote is taken. The assembly simply signifies approval by acclamation—applause, cheers, and the like. Also, the person who starts the meeting doesn't have to nominate someone. The temporary chair might instead state:

> **The meeting will please come to order. Will someone nominate a chair?**

After receiving a nomination, it should be put to a vote as described above. In a large, formal assembly, the person who does the nominating and one other member often escort the new presiding officer to the chair. The presiding officer then makes a short speech thanking the assembly for the honor.

Assume that Mr. Vermeer was elected chair in an ordinary meeting. The first thing he should do is see to it that a secretary is elected. He or someone else would then make a motion nominating someone for this post. After that, several names may be called out, and Mr. Vermeer would name each person nominated: "Mrs. Blumenthal is nominated, Ms. Wright is nominated, Mr. Pendleton is nominated," and so on. After naming each nominee, he would ask for a vote as follows, taking a vote on each one in the order nominated:

> **Those in favor of Mrs. Blumenthal acting as secretary of this meeting will say aye. [*Pause for the affirmative vote.*] Those opposed say no.**

If the motion is lost, a vote is requested for Ms. Wright and so on until someone is elected. Following election, the secretary should take a seat near the chair and keep a record of the proceedings (as described in Section 51).

Adoption of Resolutions. Usually, a chair and a secretary are the only two officers needed for an occasional meeting, so when the secretary is elected, the chair should immediately focus on the purpose of the meeting, as shown in these examples:

What business is there to consider?

Will Ms. Anderson please explain the purpose of this meeting?

At this point, if the meeting is merely a public assembly called together to consider some special subject, someone would offer a series of previously prepared resolutions or else move to appoint a committee to prepare them. In the first case, the exchange might resemble this:

Mr. Brent (addressing the chair): **Mr. Chairman.**

Chair (recognizing the member): **Mr. Brent.**

The member now has the floor and can make his motion:

Mr. Brent: **I move that we adopt the following resolutions** [*he reads them and hands them to the chair*].

Ms. Schott: **I second the motion.**

The chair sometimes directs the secretary to read the resolutions again and then states:

The question is on the adoption of the resolutions just read. [*No one rises or speaks immediately, so he adds this:*] **Are you ready to vote?** [*Again, no one rises or speaks, so he puts the question to a vote.*] **Those in favor of adopting the resolutions just read say aye.** [*Pause for the yes vote.*] **Those opposed say no.**

The chair then announces the result of the vote:

The motion is carried—the resolutions are adopted.

The ayes have it—the resolutions are adopted.

In legislative bodies, all resolutions, bills, and so on are sent to the clerk's desk. The title of the bill and the name of the member introducing it would be written on each one. In such bodies, however, there are several clerks and only one chair. In many assemblies, there is only one secretary, or clerk. Since that one person also has to keep the minutes, it's a mistake to keep interrupting the secretary to read every resolution offered.

In such assemblies, unless some rule or established custom requires otherwise, it's permissible and much better to hand all resolutions, reports, and so on directly to the chair. If they were read by the member introducing them and no one had asked for another reading, the chair could omit reading them again, assuming it's clear that they're fully understood. (For the manner of reading and stating a motion when a resolution has several paragraphs, see Section 44.)

Committee to Draft Resolutions. Sometimes resolutions haven't been prepared, and it's best to have a committee draft them. In that case, someone should address the chair and, after being recognized, move to appoint a committee:

I move that a committee be appointed to draft resolutions reflecting the views of this meeting on [*subject*].

After the motion is seconded the chair states the motion (see Section 65) and asks:

Are you ready for the question?

Are you ready to vote on the appointment?

If no one rises or speaks, the chair puts the motion to a vote and announces the result. Assuming that the motion carried and that it didn't specify any number of members for the committee, the chair should next ask:

How many should there be on the committee?

If only one number is suggested, the chair might simply announce that the committee will consist of that number.

If several numbers are suggested, though, the chair should state each one and take a vote on each number, starting with the largest number and continuing until one of them is approved. The chair would then inquire:

How shall the committee be appointed?

The matter of appointment is usually decided informally (no vote). The committee members might be appointed by the chair, in which case the chair would simply name the members without any vote. Or the committee members might be nominated by the chair or another member of the assembly. (A member may not name more than one person, except by unanimous consent.) The assembly would then vote on their appointment.

When the chair does the nominating, he or she states the names and puts the question to a vote concerning the entire committee:

> **Those in favor of these people constituting the committee say aye. [*Pause for the yes vote.*] Those opposed say no.**

When nominations are made by members of the assembly, more names may be mentioned than the number selected for the committee. In that case, a separate vote must be taken on each name, in the order nominated. (In a mass meeting, it's safer to have all committees appointed by the chair.)

Once a committee is appointed, the members should leave immediately, go to work, and agree on a report. This report should be written out as described in Section 53. During their absence, the assembly may take care of other business or spend the time listening to speeches.

When the chair notices the committee returning to the room, he or she should wait for anyone who is speaking to stop and then announce that the assembly is ready to hear the committee's report or resolutions. Or the chair might first ask the committee if it's ready to report.

The committee chair should take the first opportunity to obtain the floor (see Section 2). This person is the one named first to be on the committee and often is the one who earlier moved to appoint the committee. After being recognized by the assembly's presiding officer, the committee chair would state:

> **The committee appointed to draft the resolutions is ready to report.**

The presiding officer would then state that the assembly "will now hear the report." The committee chair would read the report and hand it to the presiding officer. At that moment, the committee is automatically dissolved without any action by the assembly.

Someone in the assembly should next move to adopt or accept the report or to agree to the resolutions. Any such motion has the same effect. If it carries, the resolutions prepared by the committee become the resolutions of the assembly just as if the committee had nothing to do with them. (See Section 30 for common errors in acting on reports.)

After someone makes a motion to adopt (see Section 53) or accept the report or agree to the resolutions, the presiding officer states the motion to and puts it to a vote as described earlier. It isn't necessary to adopt the resolutions immediately, however. The assembly, in fact, may want to debate them, modify them, postpone consideration of them, or do something else (see Sections 55–63).

When all business that the assembly met to handle is finished or when there's another reason to close the meeting, someone should move to Adjourn (Section 11). If the motion carries and no other time for meeting again is set, the chair should state:

> **The motion is carried. This assembly stands adjourned without day.**

Another method for conducting a meeting is shown in Section 48.

Additional Officers. Perhaps more officers are needed than only a chair and secretary. They can be appointed in the manner described for the chair and secretary. Or the assembly can first form a temporary organization by electing a chairman pro tem and a secretary pro tem. As soon as a secretary pro tem is elected, then, a committee should be appointed to nominate the permanent officers (e.g., in a convention; see Section 47).

The presiding officer is usually called the president, and sometimes numerous vice-presidents are appointed merely for complimentary purposes. In large, formal meetings, these vice-presidents sit on the platform next to the president. When the president is away or gives up the chair, the first person on the list of vice-presidents who is present should take the chair.

Note: Readers who are pressed for time could, for now, skip Sections 47 through 53 and continue reading at Section 54.)

Section 47. Meeting of a Convention or Assembly of Delegates

Sometimes members of an assembly are elected or appointed to *attend* a meeting. It's necessary then to find out who is actually a member and is entitled to vote before the permanent organization is formed. First, as described in Section 46, a temporary organization is formed by electing a chairman pro tem and a secretary pro tem. The chairman pro tem then announces:

The next order of business is the appointment of a committee on credentials.

Someone then makes a motion to that effect:

I move that a committee of three on the credentials of members be appointed by the chair and that the committee report as soon as possible.

Or the motion might be less detailed:

I move that a committee of three be appointed on the credentials of members.

Either way, the chairman pro tem proceeds as described in the material about committees to draft resolutions (see Section 46).

When the time comes to vote on a motion to accept

the committee's report, the only persons who may vote are those that the committee reports as having proper credentials. The committee may do more than list the members with proper credentials (fulfilling the voting requirements). It may also report doubtful or contested cases, with recommendations about them that the assembly may adopt, reject, postpone, or handle otherwise. But only the members who have an undisputed right to their seats may vote at this time.

After the assembly disposes of the credentials question, at least temporarily, the chairman pro tem states:

The next order of business is the election of permanent officers.

Someone then moves to appoint a committee to nominate the officers. For example:

I move that a committee of three be appointed by the chairman pro tem to nominate permanent officers.

If the motion carries, the appointed committee will meet to prepare a report. As soon as the committee makes its report, someone should move for its adoption:

I move that the report of the committee be adopted and that the officers nominated be declared the officers of the [*name of body*].

When members are competing for the offices, however, it's better to elect the officers by ballot. In this case, after the nominating committee reports, someone could make a motion as in the following examples (see Section 38 for balloting and other methods of voting):

I move that the [*name of body*] now proceed to the balloting for its permanent officers.

I move that we now proceed to the election, by ballot, of the permanent officers of this [*name of body*].

The articles of incorporation, charters, or constitutions of permanent organizations may require that the officers be elected by ballot. If the motion to proceed to the election carries, the chairman pro tem immediately calls the new presiding officer to the chair. The temporary secretary is replaced at the same time, and the assembly is then ready for its work.

Section 48. A Permanent Society

First Meeting. When one or more persons want to form a permanent organization, they should see to it that only the appropriate interested persons are invited to be present at a certain time and place. Usually, in mass meetings or meetings called to organize the new body, one waits ten to fifteen minutes after the appointed time. Then someone steps forward and states:

The meeting will please come to order. I move that [*name*] act as chair of the meeting.

Someone seconds the motion, and the person who made the motion puts it to a vote (see Section 46). If, for example, Ms. Channing is elected as chair, she then announces that the election of a secretary is the first order of business.

After the secretary is elected, the chair calls on the person most interested in forming the organization to state the purpose of the meeting, or that person may make the first move:

Mr. Jacobs (*addressing the chair*): Madam Chairman.

Chair (*recognizing the member*): Mr. Jacobs.

Mr. Jacobs: We're meeting here today to discuss the formation of a new organization . . .

The chair might also ask others to give their opinions, and sometimes the members themselves call for a certain person to comment. The chair should note the wishes of the assembly but, without being too strict, should also be certain that someone doesn't speak so long that the other members become tired and impatient.

When enough time has been spent, informally, in listening to comments, someone should offer a resolution so that definite action can be taken. Those persons who want to get the meeting underway, especially if it's going to be a large meeting, should have previously agreed on what they want done. They should be ready, at the proper time, to offer a suitable resolution:

> **RESOLVED, That it is the expressed opinion of this meeting that an organization for [*purpose*] should now be formed in this city.**

This resolution would be seconded and stated by the chair. It then is open to debate and should be voted on as described earlier (see Section 46). If the meeting is very large, it might be better to offer the resolution at the start of the meeting and skip the informal discussion.

After voting on the above motion, or even before that motion is offered, someone may propose the following:

> **I move that a committee of five be appointed by the chair to draft the charter and the bylaws for an organization for [*purpose*] and that they report at an adjourned meeting of this assembly.**

This motion may be amended (see Section 56) by striking out and adding words and so on. It's also debatable.

When the committee to draft the charter and the bylaws is appointed, the chair may ask something such as this:

> **Is there any other business to discuss?**

When all business is finished, someone should move to adjourn to meet at a certain place and time (see Section 10). This motion, however, after being seconded and stated by the chair, is open to debate and amendment. A better alternative, therefore, might be to fix the time of the next meeting earlier in the proceedings. Then, when business is finished, someone can move simply to Adjourn (Section 11), which by itself can't be amended or debated. If the motion to Adjourn carries, the chair should state:

> **This meeting stands adjourned to meet at [*time and place*].**

Second Meeting. Ordinary meetings of organized groups are conducted like the second meeting (the chair, however, always announces business in the order specified in the organization's rules [see Section 44]). At the second meeting, the officers of the previous meeting still serve (if present) until new permanent officers are elected.

When it's time to start the meeting, the chair from the previous meeting stands (in a formal setting) and states:

> **The meeting will please come to order.**

As soon as the people are seated and quiet, he or she adds:

> **The secretary will read the minutes of the last meeting.**

If someone notices an error in the minutes, that person should point it out as soon as the secretary finishes reading. If no one objects, the chair can simply direct the secretary to make the correction without waiting for someone to make such a motion. After that, the chair would state:

> **If there's no objection, the minutes will stand approved as read [*or* "corrected," *if that's the case*].**

The chair would then announce the next item on the agenda, for example:

> **The next order of business is hearing reports from the standing committees.**

The chair may ask each committee, in proper order, to make a report:

Does the Membership [*or other*] Committee have a report to make?

The committee will either report or state that it has nothing to report. Since some or even all of the committees may have nothing to report, the chair could save time by asking generally:

Do any committees have reports to make?

If no one rises to report, the chair could then move on:

Since there are no reports from the standing committees, the next item will be to hear reports of select committees.

The same procedure can be followed in asking select committees for reports. At every meeting, the chair should have a list of the committees to use in calling on them for reports and also as a guide in appointing new committees.

Perhaps some committee, such as the Bylaws Committee, will want to report at the meeting. The committee chair would address the presiding officer of the assembly (Mr. or Madam Chairman) and, after being recognized, would read the report and then hand it to the presiding officer. If no one makes a motion, the presiding officer should ask what the assembly wants to do, as shown in these examples:

You've heard the report read—what shall we do with it [*or "what shall be done with it"*]?

You've heard the report read—what action shall we take on it?

In large, formal meetings, the chair would usually ask the secretary to read the report again before asking what to do with it. (See Section 30 for common errors in acting on reports; see also Section 46.)

In an ordinary assembly, someone would move to adopt it at this time or, using the preceding example, would move "to adopt the charter reported by the committee." (An organization that is incorporated must be set up according to the laws of the particular state. Therefore, its articles of incorporation, charter, or constitution is usually prepared or reviewed by an attorney. Amendments also would then require the approval of legal counsel.)

After this motion is seconded, the presiding officer of the assembly should state the question:

The question is on the adoption of the charter reported by the committee.

He or she would then read the first article and ask:

Are there any amendments proposed to this article?

If none is offered, the chair would go on to the next article and so on until each one has been read and made available for amendment. (If articles are subdivided into sections or paragraphs, the amendments also should be made by sections or paragraphs.) The entire document would then be open for amendment:

The whole charter, having been read, is open to amendment.

Anyone is free at that time to move to amend any part of the document. When the chair believes everyone is finished, he or she should ask:

Are you ready for the question?

Are you ready to vote?

If no one wants to speak, the chair will assume that the assembly is ready and will put the question to a vote:

Those in favor of adopting the charter as

> amended say aye. [*Pause for yes vote.*] Those
> opposed say no.

The chair should announce the result of the vote
distinctly.

If the assembly voted to adopt the charter as
amended, the chair immediately should state that it has
been adopted and those who want to become members
must sign it (and pay any initiation fee required by the
document).

If the assembly is large, the chair may suggest a recess
to give people time to sign. Someone could move to take
a recess for ten (or other) minutes or until the document
is signed. Once it is signed, no one may vote at this
meeting except those who signed it.

After the recess, the chair must call the meeting to
order again and state the next item to handle:

> **The next order of business is the adoption of
> the bylaws.**

Someone should then move to adopt the bylaws reported by the committee, with the chair following the
same steps as those for adopting the charter. Afterward,
the chair should ask about further business, as shown in
these examples:

> **Is there any further business?**
>
> **Is there any further business to come before
> this meeting?**

Or the chair might simply state that the next item of
business is the election of permanent officers of the
organization.

If that's the next order of business, someone should
move to appoint a committee to nominate the permanent officers (see Section 47 for handling such a motion).
As each officer is elected, he or she replaces the temporary officer. When they're all elected, the organization
of the new entity is considered to be completed.

Section 49. Constitutions, Bylaws, Rules of Order, and Standing Rules

In preparing the articles of incorporation, charter, or constitution and the bylaws, it's always a good idea to get copies of the ones used by similar organizations. The committee appointed to prepare (with or without an attorney) the documents can then compare the copies and select the most appropriate one to use as a guide, amending each article of it (or each section or paragraph) just as the assembly will eventually amend the committee's report.

After the committee has amended the charter it chose to use as a guide (see Section 48), it should adopt it as amended and go on to the bylaws, treating the bylaws the same way. After the committee is finished with both documents, someone should move to return to the assembly:

> **I move that the committee rise and that the [*committee*] chair [*or another member*] report the charter and the bylaws to the assembly.**

If this motion passes, the documents are written out, and a brief report is made:

> **The committee, appointed to draft a charter and bylaws, respectfully submits the following, with the recommendation that they be adopted as the charter and the bylaws of this organization.**

The material offered may be signed by all of the committee members who agree with the reported version or just by the committee chair.

In the above example, it's assumed that both a charter and bylaws are adopted. Some organizations, however, have only one document. When a group adopts both, the charter may contain only the following:

- Name and purpose of the society

- Qualification of members

- Officers and their election and duties

- Meetings of the organization (but only including what is essential, such as general voting requirements, and leaving miscellaneous details for the bylaws)

- How to amend the document

The five items can be arranged in five articles, with each article divided into various sections. Since this document has only fundamental information, an organization should make it very difficult to amend. Usually, an organization requires previous notice of any proposed amendment and a two-thirds or three-fourths vote to adopt it (see Section 45); it's a good idea not to require a larger vote than two-thirds.

When a group has frequent meetings, it shouldn't make an amendment to the document except at a quarterly or annual meeting. Even then, it should do so only after proposing the amendment at the previous quarterly meeting.

The bylaws should contain all of the other rules of an organization that are too important to be changed without giving prior notice to all members about the proposed change, although the most important rules may be placed in the articles of incorporation, charter, or constitution rather than in the bylaws.

The bylaws might omit the rules about the conduct of business in a meeting and collect such rules in a separate document: the rules of order. In any case, every organization should have one rule in particular—either in its bylaws or in the rules of order:

> **The rules contained in [*name a selected book on parliamentary practice*] shall govern the organization in all cases to which they are applicable and in which they are not inconsistent with the rules of order [*or bylaws*] of this organization.**

Without a rule to that effect, someone could cause a lot of trouble in a meeting.

Standing rules are occasionally adopted by an organization in addition to its articles of incorporation, charter, or constitution, as well as its bylaws and rules of order. Such rules are permanent resolutions that are binding on the organization until rescinded or modified. Standing rules can be adopted by a majority vote at any meeting. No standing rule (or other resolution), though, can be adopted if it's in conflict with the articles of incorporation, charter, or constitution or the bylaws or rules of order.

Once standing rules have been adopted, they can't be modified during the same session except by a motion to Reconsider (Sections 27, 60) them. But they can be suspended, modified, or rescinded by a majority vote at any future session.

Standing rules, then, are rules that are adopted like ordinary resolutions with no need to give previous notice (required for bylaws). Members at any future session, therefore, may terminate them.

The various types of rules are, unfortunately, mixed in some organizations, and that causes confusion. In other words, the standing rules really may be the bylaws if an organization doesn't allow them to be suspended or doesn't allow them to be amended without previous notice.

Mixing the classes of rules is a mistake. Standing rules should contain only those rules that are subject to the will of the majority at any meeting and those rules that it may want to change at any time (without having to give prior notice). Rules of order, on the other hand, should consist of only the rules pertaining to the orderly transaction of business at a meeting.

The rules of order and, subject to any legal requirements, the bylaws and the articles of incorporation, charter, or constitution should contain some provision for their own amendment. The rules of order should also provide for their own suspension. The bylaws, too, might have a provision allowing for certain articles to be suspended (see Section 18).

Article X. Officers and Committees

Section 50. Chairman or President

The chair's duties include the following:

- To call the meeting to order at the appointed time

- To preside at all of the meetings

- To announce business before the assembly in its proper order

- To state and put to a vote all motions that are properly brought before the assembly.

- To preserve order and proper behavior

- To decide all questions of order (subject to an appeal; see Section 14)

If you're conducting the proceedings before a large assembly, when you put a motion to a vote or speak in response to an appeal, you should stand; in all other cases, you may remain seated. In meetings of boards, committees, and other small groups, though, the chair usually doesn't stand, and even members who are speaking keep their seats.

When you're conducting a meeting, you should observe these rules as well:

- Whenever a vote by the chair would affect the result or when the assembly is voting by ballot, the chair may vote also.

- When someone stands to speak and addresses you as chair (Mr. or Madam Chairman), respond by stating the person's name, if known, or by nodding to acknowledge the person.

- Don't interrupt a speaker as long as the person is in order but rather listen to the speech (which should be addressed to the chair and not the assembly).

- Be careful not to appear to take sides while conducting a meeting, but you may call another member to take the chair while you address the meeting.

- Don't leave the chair while routinely speaking on a motion or a matter of order.

People inexperienced in conducting a meeting should thoroughly study their organization's articles of incorporation, charter, or constitution and its bylaws and rules of order in advance, taking copies along while occupying the chair. A presiding officer also needs to be able to answer members who ask what motion to make concerning some matter before the assembly (see Section 55).

It's a good idea for a chair to memorize the list of ordinary motions in their order of precedence and to become completely familiar with the table of rules (see list and table in the Quick-Reference Guide). The table can be scanned quickly during a meeting when you need to look up something you don't know offhand.

In addition, the chair needs to know all of the business that normally comes before a meeting and call for it in its regular or assigned order. Since it may be necessary to appoint new committees, the chair should also bring along a list of the members of all committees already existing.

Whenever someone makes a motion and it's seconded, immediately and distinctly state the motion to the assembly:

> **The question is whether the chair should appoint a conference committee.**

After a vote is taken, announce the result ("The ayes have it—the motion is carried") and state what other motion, if any, is pending at that time (see Section 54 for the proper form). But don't wait for routine motions to be seconded when you know that no one objects to them (see Section 65).

Sometimes a member unknowingly makes an improper motion. In that case, politely suggest the proper motion.

> *Example:* Suppose that someone moves to table a motion (see Section 19) until a certain time. Since that's an incorrect motion, ask the person if he or she means to Postpone [the matter] to a Certain Time (Section 21). If the member says yes, announce that "the question is on postponement to [*time*]." On the other hand, if someone moves simply "to postpone the matter" without stating a time, don't rule it out of

order. But do ask the person if he or she wants to move to Postpone [the matter] Indefinitely (Section 24), which would kill it, or to Lay [the matter] on the Table, which means that it can be taken up at any other time. After the person tells you what he or she means, state the motion that way.

Example: Suppose that after a report has been presented and read, someone moves that "it be received." Ask if the person means to move "to adopt" or "to accept" it, since the report has already been received. (No vote is taken on *receiving* a report since that merely brings it before the assembly and allows it to be read—unless someone objects to receiving it; see Section 30.)

Although a committee chair usually has more to say than the other committee members, the chair of an ordinary assembly, especially a large one, has the least to say of all members concerning the merits of pending questions. But the chair, nevertheless, controls the assembly in a fair and just manner.

As chair, you would never interrupt members who are speaking simply because you know more about some matter than they do. Moreover, you would never let yourself get excited or respond unfairly to even the most troublesome member. Nor would you take advantage of someone's ignorance of parliamentary law even when you might temporarily accomplish something good by doing so.

As chair, you would need to know all about parliamentary procedure but shouldn't try to show off your knowledge. You should be careful not to be more technical or strict than is absolutely necessary for the good of the meeting.

Above all, you should use your own best judgment in all situations. For example, perhaps an assembly would be hindered, not helped, by a strict enforcement of the rules. But in large assemblies, in which there's a lot to do and always the potential for trouble, you would likely find that the safest course is to insist that the rules be strictly observed.

Section 51. The Clerk, Secretary, or Recording Secretary

The titles clerk, secretary, and recording secretary all refer to the same person. This individual keeps a record of the proceedings (minutes) at each meeting. How detailed the record must be depends on the type of meeting. In an occasional or mass meeting, for example, the record is usually very brief. But in any meeting, the secretary should always record every resolution or motion that's adopted.

For a large meeting, it's often a good idea to keep a full record of the proceedings for publication. If the meeting lasts for several days, it's best to appoint one or more assistants to help.

Deciding what to record can be a difficult task. Sometimes the main points of each speech should be written down. In other cases, it may be enough to write that a matter was discussed by so and so in the affirmative and by so and so in the negative.

Every adopted resolution must be recorded in full, for example:

> **On the motion of Mr. Benson, it was resolved that . . .**

Sometimes the topics at a large meeting are assigned beforehand to certain speakers who make formal speeches. When a speaker finishes his or her subject, it's then open for discussion. People who want to discuss a subject will have some time limit, such as five minutes, to respond to the speaker's address.

In such cases, the minutes can be very brief—unless they're going to be published. Then they'll have to include either the full addresses of the speakers or carefully prepared abstracts. Such detailed minutes would also have to show the drift of the members' responses to each subject.

In a permanent organization, when the minutes aren't published, they consist of a record of what was done, not what was said. The recorded version is then kept in a minutes book or file.

The secretary who keeps the minutes, regardless of detail, should never use them personally to make any criticism or any favorable remarks about what was said or done in a meeting.

Informal minutes might be prepared in a form such as that shown here (see also Chapter 8 in the first part of the book on meeting arrangements):

> *Example:* At a regular meeting of the XYZ Society, held in its hall, on Thursday evening, March 16, 19XX, with Ms. Addington presiding and Mr. Steinberg acting as secretary, the minutes of the previous meeting were read and approved. The Applications Committee reported the names of Jane Worley and Geoffrey Reynolds as applicants for membership. On the motion of Mr. Brighton, they were admitted as members. The Budget Committee reported through Ms. Purl two resolutions that were thoroughly discussed, amended, and adopted, as follows:
>
> RESOLVED, That . . .
>
> RESOLVED, That . . .
>
> On the motion of Mrs. Harrison, the society adjourned.
>
> **Marilyn Foster, Secretary**

When proceedings must be published, it's a good idea to examine the published proceedings of other similar meetings and to try to conform to the established style or custom, except when it's clearly improper to do so (see Chapter 8 in the first part of the book on meeting arrangements).

Put the articles of incorporation, charter, or constitution and the bylaws, rules of order, and standing rules all in one place. When an article is amended, include the date of amendment in the revised version.

It's the secretary's job to keep all papers belonging to the organization that aren't specifically the responsibility of, or assigned for safekeeping to, some other officer, such as the treasurer. However, the secretary sometimes has financial duties, too (see Section 52).

Section 52. Treasurer

The treasurer's duties vary from one group to another. The treasurer may act like a banker and merely hold the funds the organization receives and pay bills signed by the secretary. The treasurer's annual report (always required) would then be merely a statement of the amount on hand at the beginning of the year, the amount received during the year (stating the sources of the money), the total amount paid out, and the balance on hand.

This report next goes to the Auditing Committee, which consists of one or two persons. They examine the treasurer's books and vouchers and certify on the report that they have examined the accounts and vouchers and find them correct and that the balance on hand is so and so (stating the precise amount). When the Auditing Committee's report is accepted, it's the equivalent of a resolution by the organization to the same effect—namely, that the treasurer's report is correct.

In the situation just described, the real financial statement would be made either by a board, the secretary, or some other officer, according to the requirements stated in the organization's articles of incorporation, charter, or constitution. The idea behind all of this is that any officer who receives money on behalf of an organization must account for it in a report, and the officer who's responsible for the disbursements must also report them to the organization.

If the secretary is the one responsible for the expenses, which is the case in many organizations, and the treasurer simply pays out on the secretary's order, the secretary should also be the one who makes a report of the expenses. This report should be prepared using appropriate expenses categories so that the organization can easily see which things the various amounts of money were spent on.

The main purpose of a financial report, then, is to give members the information they want or are entitled to have. But all of the details, such as specific dates or separate checks written for the same purpose, would simply clutter a report and make it difficult to understand. The Auditing Committee, not all individual members of the organization, is meant to examine such details.

Since an officer has to account for any money spent, it's important always to get a receipt for any payment. Keep such receipts in regular order, since they'll serve as the vouchers to be examined by the Auditing Committee. You can't be too careful where someone else's money is concerned. In fact, officers should *insist* on having their accounts audited every time they make a report so that any errors will be caught and quickly corrected.

Once an organization accepts an Auditing Committee's statement that a financial report is correct, the officer who made the payments is relieved of responsibility for past accounting. In other words, if the payment vouchers were to get lost, it's not a problem in terms of past responsibility.

To decide what form of financial report to use for your organization, look at those prepared in similar organizations. The example below can be varied to suit most cases.

Treasurer's Report

The undersigned, treasurer of XYZ Club, hereby submits the following annual report:

The balance on hand at the beginning of the year was _____ dollars and _____ cents. There was received from all sources during the year _____ dollars and _____ cents; during the same time the expenses amounted to _____ dollars and _____ cents, leaving a balance on hand of _____ dollars and _____ cents.

The attached statement of receipts and expenditures will show in detail the sources of receipts and the items to which the expenditures were applied.

David Eggert
Treasurer, XYZ Club

You can make a Statement of Receipts and Expenditures simply by listing the receipts, followed by the expenses, and ending with the balance on hand.

Balance on hand, Jan. 1, 19XX		**$ 991.13**
Receipts		
Member dues	860.00	
Initiation fees	95.00	
Fines	15.00	
Total Receipts		970.00
Total		1,961.13
Expenditures		
Room rental	500.00	
Gas	80.00	
Stationery	26.50	
Cleaning service	360.00	
Total Expenditures		966.50
Total		$ 994.63
Balance on hand, Dec. 31, 19XX		**$ 994.63**

> [Signature]
> David Eggert
> Treasurer

The Auditing Committee's certification about the correctness of the account may be written on, or attached to, the statement, for example:

> **We do hereby certify that we have examined the accounts and vouchers of the treasurer and find them to be correct and that the balance in the account is nine hundred and ninety-four dollars and sixty-three cents ($994.63).**
>
> **FOR THE AUDITING COMMITTEE**
> **Jennifer Randal**_____
> **Lewis Samson**_____

Section 53. Committees

Committees may not be needed in small meetings, especially if there is little business to transact. But in large meetings with a lot to do, committees are very important. When a committee is selected properly, its action will probably decide the action of the entire assembly.

A committee set up for action should be small and consist only of people who wholeheartedly support a proposed action. But a committee set up for deliberation or investigation should be larger. It should represent all of the parties or all sides of a matter so that its opinion will carry as much weight as possible. If some faction is left out or underrepresented, the committee won't be as useful. (See Section 46 on the appointment of a committee.)

The committee chair is the first person named to be on a committee. This person calls the committee together and presides at its meetings. Or a majority of the committee members may elect someone else to serve as chair, provided that the assembly hasn't already appointed the chair for them.

If the committee chair is absent or simply fails or refuses to call a meeting, any other two members can call the members together for a meeting. Since the committee is a miniature assembly, it can act only when a quorum (see Section 43) is present.

When a paper is referred to a committee, the members must not write on it. Amendments by the committee should be written on a separate sheet. If the paper originates in the committee, though, and doesn't come from the assembly, all of the amendments by the committee must be incorporated in the paper.

Usually, when a committee prepares a paper, someone from the committee drafts it in advance of the committee meeting. The draft is then read paragraph by paragraph. After each one, the committee chair asks:

Are there any amendments to this paragraph?

The committee doesn't vote to adopt each paragraph as it comes up but rather waits until the whole paper has been covered (paragraph by paragraph). Then the paper as a whole is also open to amendment, and at that time the committee members can strike out any paragraph, insert new paragraphs, or even substitute an entirely new paper. As soon as the paper has been amended to suit the committee, the members should adopt it as their report and ask the committee chair, or some other member, to report it to the assembly.

The entire paper should be written out, with the opening resembling one of these examples:

The committee to which [*subject*] was referred submits the following report.

Your committee appointed to [*purpose*] respectfully reports as follows.

At the end of the report would be a closing ("Respectfully submitted"), followed by the signatures of all committee members who support the report or, perhaps, by only the signature of the committee chair.

Sometimes the minority on a committee submits a separate report. It might start by stating:

The undersigned, a minority of the committee appointed to [*purpose*], respectfully submits the following report.

The minority usually presents its report after the committee's report has been read. But the only way an assembly can act on a minority report is to move to substitute it for the report of the committee.

Once the committee's report has been read, the committee is automatically discharged without any need for a motion to that effect. However, the committee could be revived if someone would make a motion (and the assembly would adopt it) to refer (recommit) the paper back to the same committee.

Article XI. Introduction of Business

Section 54. How to Introduce Business

If you want to bring up some matter at a meeting, write it down (unless it's very simple) in the form of a motion, for example:

> **RESOLVED That the thanks of this convention be expressed to the citizens of this community for their hearty welcome and generous hospitality.**

At the proper moment—when no other business is before the assembly—stand up (in a large assembly) and address the chair by title (Mr. Chairman, Madam President, and so on). The chair should immediately recognize you, announcing your name (if known to the chair) or otherwise simply nodding to acknowledge you (it helps if members state their names right after addressing the chair). This means that you have the floor and can make your motion:

> **I move that we adopt the following resolution.**

Or you might state that you want to "offer" the following resolution, read it, and then move that it be adopted. If the assembly is large, your name should be written on the resolution, especially if a lot of other business is being transacted at the meeting.

As soon as you've finished, hand your written resolution to the chair. Someone will second the motion (or the chair will ask if there's a second), and the chair will state the motion:

> **It has been moved and seconded that the following resolution be adopted [*reads resolution*].**

Or the chair could first read it and then state the motion:

> **The question is on the adoption of the resolution just read.**

That statement opens the resolution to discussion. Anyone who wants to speak, though, must first obtain the floor in the usual manner (address the chair and wait to be recognized).

But perhaps no one will rise ro speak. At any rate, as soon as the chair thinks debate is closed, he or she asks:

> **Are you ready for the question [*or* "Is there any further discussion"; see Section 65]?**

Again, if no one rises or speaks, the chair puts the question to a vote in a form similar to this:

> **The question is on the adoption of the resolution just read. Those in favor of its adoption say aye. [*Pause for yes vote.*] Those opposed say no.**

After the no votes are in, the chair should announce the result, stating that the motion is carried or lost. If it carried, the chair might reply as in one of these examples:

> **The motion is carried—the resolution is adopted.**

> **The ayes have it—the resolution is adopted.**

A majority of the votes cast is enough to adopt any motion except those identified in Section 39. (For other forms of stating motions and putting them to a vote, see Section 65; for other illustrations of the common practice in introducing business and in making various motions, see Sections 46–48.)

Article XII. Motions

Section 55. Motions Classified According to Their Object

Instead of adopting or rejecting a resolution immediately, the members might want to dispose of it in some other way. Certain motions can be used for this purpose while a resolution is being considered, and for the time being, those motions must be acted on first (if they qualify as taking precedence over the resolution; see list of precedence of motions in the Quick-Reference Guide). But no one may make any of these motions while someone else has the floor, except as shown in the table of rules (see Quick-Reference Guide).

Once a motion has been recognized by the chair as pending, it has to be disposed of by a vote, unless the mover withdraws it or unless the assembly adjourns while it's pending. It may be interrupted, however, by any motions that have precedence over it. But once those other motions have been acted on, the members must resume consideration of the pending question (unless one of the other motions in effect settled the original matter under consideration).

No new motion is necessary to bring back a pending question before the assembly. The members simply return to it as soon as other motions that interrupted it are taken care of.

The following list shows most of the motions that can be made while another matter is pending. The motions are arranged here in eight categories according to the reason for wanting to make the motion.

Objective	*Motions to Accomplish Objective*
To modify or amend (see Section 56)	To Amend (Section 23)
	To Commit or Refer (Section 22)
To defer action (see Section 57)	To Postpone to a Certain Time (Section 21)
	To Lay on the Table (Section 19)
To suppress debate (see Section 58)	To call for the Previous Question (Section 20)
	To Limit Debate or Close Debate (Section 37)
To suppress the question (see Section 59)	To Object to Consideration of a Question (Section 15)

	To Postpone Indefinitely (Section 24)
	To Lay on the Table (Section 19)
To consider a question the second time (see Section 60)	To Reconsider (Section 27)
To apply orders and rules (see Section 61)	To call for Orders of the Day (Section 13)
	To make a Special Order (Section 13)
	To Suspend the Rules (Section 18)
	To raise Questions of Order (Sections 14, 61)
	To Appeal (Section 14)
To handle miscellaneous maters (see Section 62)	To request Reading of Papers (Section 16)
	To Withdraw a Motion (Section 17)
	To raise Questions of Privilege (Section 12)
To close a meeting (see Section 63)	To Fix the Time to Which to Adjourn (Section 10)
	To Adjourn (Section 11)

Section 56. To Modify or Amend

To amend. If you want to modify a motion, you would make another motion to Amend (Section 23) it by one of these means:

- To add words

- To strike out words

- To strike out certain words and insert others

- To substitute a different motion on the same subject for the one currently before the assembly

- To divide the motion into two or more motions to get a separate vote on some particular point(s)

Sometimes the opponents of a measure try to amend it in such a way that the proponents will become divided over it, thereby causing defeat of the measure.

When a motion for an amendment has been made and seconded, the chair should state the motion distinctly so that the members will know exactly what decision they have to make. The chair, therefore, should first read the paragraphs being amended, next the words to be taken out (if any), then the words to be inserted (if any), and, finally, the paragraph as it will read if the proposed amendment is adopted.

As soon as the chair finishes reading an amendment, he or she should state that the question is on the adoption of the amendment and is open to debate. Comments at this point should be confined to the merits of the amendment and shouldn't concern the main motion being amended unless it's necessary to discuss it to decide if the amendment should be adopted.

The amendment itself can also be amended. But an amendment of an amendment can't be amended further. In other words, an amendment can itself be amended only once.

None of the undebatable motions (see Section 35) can be amended except to Fix the Time to Which to Adjourn (Section 10), to Extend the Limits of Debate (Section 34), and to Close Debate or to Limit Debate (Section 37). The motion to Postpone [a matter] Indefinitely (Section 24) also cannot be amended.

To Commit or Refer. Sometimes the original motion is very complex, or perhaps it needs a more extensive amendment than the assembly can make. In such cases, someone should move to Commit or Refer (Section 22) it to a committee. You can make such a motion while an amendment is pending, and it opens up the whole merits of the question to debate.

You also could amend the motion to Commit or Refer something by specifying the number of the committee, how the members will be appointed, when they'll report, or by giving any other instructions. (See Section 53 on committees and Section 46 on their appointment.)

Section 57. To Defer Action

To Postpone to a Certain Time. If you want to defer action on something until a particular time, the proper motion is to postpone it to that time. The motion to Postpone [the matter] to a Certain Time (Section 21) allows only limited debate, and it has to be confined to the pros and cons of postponement to the specified time. You can make this motion while another motion to Amend, to Commit, or to Postpone Indefinitely is pending.

You could amend a motion postponing something to another time by changing the time; that amendment, though, would allow only the same limited debate. If you propose another time, it may not be beyond the *current* session (see Section 42); it may, however, be postponed to the *next* regular business session, at which time it will come up with the unfinished business and consequently take precedence over new business on that day (see Section 44).

To Lay on the Table. Instead of postponing a matter until a particular time, you might want to lay it aside temporarily while dealing with something else but still reserve the right to consider the matter at any time. In Congress, the motion to Lay [a matter] on the Table (Section 19) is commonly used to defeat a measure. A majority, however, may take it up again at any other time.

Some organizations won't allow a tabled motion to be taken up again except by a two-thirds vote to do so. Such a rule really deprives the group of the advantages of being able to table something. It wouldn't be safe to lay something aside temporarily because it might not be possible to get a two-thirds vote later to take it up again. A one-third minority, in fact, could easily dispose of a measure it didn't like by tabling it, knowing it would be unlikely that a two-thirds vote would be available later to call it back.

In ordinary groups, a bare majority shouldn't have the

power to adopt or reject something or to prevent others from considering it without debate. (See Section 35 on the principles involved in making motions undebatable.)

In any case, the way to put something aside temporarily is to move that the matter be laid on the table. Since neither debate nor amendment is allowed on that motion, the chair would immediately put the motion to a vote. If it passed, the matter would be set aside until the assembly voted to take it from the table.

The motion to Take [a subject] from the Table (Section 19) can't be amended, can't be debated, and doesn't have precedence over any other motions. Moreover, an affirmative vote on it can't be reconsidered. Sometimes this motion, too, is used to suppress a measure, as shown in Section 59.

Section 58. To Suppress Debate

Motions to suppress debate are strictly for closing or limiting debate. They may be used by either friends or foes of a measure. Opponents of a measure could also close debate on it by suppressing the question being debated (see Section 59).

Previous Question. If you want to force action on a debatable question, all you have to do is obtain the floor and call for the Previous Question (Section 20). After the call is seconded, the chair has to put the matter to a vote right away because a call for the Previous Question can't be debated:

Shall the main question be now put?

Shall the main question be put to a vote?

After asking for yes and no votes, if this motion for the Previous Question passes by a two-thirds vote (see Section 39), all debate on the main motion stops immediately, unless a committee member is in the midst of reporting the pending measure; anyone who thus has the floor is entitled to close the debate.

As soon as debate stops, the chair puts the question to the assembly. If a motion to Commit (Section 22) a resolution or other matter is pending, the chair first puts that to a vote. If that motion carries, the subject goes to the committee; if it fails, the next vote is taken on any amendments and, finally, on the matter as amended.

Suppose that the pending motion is one to Postpone [a matter] Indefinitely (Section 24), to Postpone [a matter] to a Certain Time (Section 21), to Reconsider (Section 27) the matter, or to make an Appeal (Section 14). Then the Previous Question is exhausted (no longer applies or has any effect) by a vote on a postponement, a reconsideration, or an appeal; that is, the Previous Questions, in that case, would no longer apply and, therefore, wouldn't cut off debate on any other motions that might be pending.

Suppose, however, that the call for the Previous Question fails. If it does, the debate simply continues as though the motion calling for the Previous Question had never been made.

You can also call for the Previous Question on an amendment. In that case, after the vote is taken on the amendment, the main motion is once more open to debate. (Since the use of the Previous Question is often misunderstood, reread Section 20 for further clarification.)

To Limit or Close Debate. Assume that you don't want to end debate completely. Then you wouldn't call for the Previous Question because that would stop everything and bring the matter to a vote. To simply limit debate (see Section 37), not kill it entirely, you can move to limit the time each person may speak or to limit the number of speeches on each side of an issue, pro and con. Or you can move to appoint a time when debate must close and the matter has to be put to a vote.

You also can move to limit debate on an amendment or on an amendment to an amendment. Afterward, then, the main motion being amended would still be open to continuing debate and further amendment.

In ordinary organizations, where harmony is so important, a two-thirds vote should be required on any motion to cut off or limit debate. (The House requires only a majority vote to pass these motions. The Senate, on the other hand, doesn't even recognize motions to close or limit debate.)

Section 59. To Suppress the Question

Objection to the Consideration of a Question. Sometimes a resolution is introduced in an assembly that the members don't want to consider. Perhaps it's irrelevant to the objectives of the group or simply wouldn't be worth the time needed to deal with it. Whatever the reason, if you don't want to spend time on something, you should make a motion to the effect that you object to considering the matter.

An Objection to Consideration of a Question (Section 15) doesn't require a second, so the chair would immediately put this motion to a vote:

Will the assembly consider this question?

Should the objection be sustained?

After asking for yes and no votes, the chair would announce the result. If the members, by a two-thirds vote, decide they don't want to consider the matter, it is dismissed right away and can't be introduced again during the current session.

A key requirement in objecting to the consideration of a question is that it be done when the matter is first introduced, before it has been debated. You can make your motion to Reconsider something even though someone else has the floor.

To Postpone Indefinitely. Once a matter has been debated, there are two ways you can suppress it: defeat it with a no vote or move to Postpone [it] Indefinitely (Section 24). Both have the same effect. Even if the motion to Postpone [a matter] Indefinitely should be lost, there's still a chance to defeat the matter after an amendment to it has been voted on. Although you can't move to Postpone [a matter] Indefinitely when another motion (other than the original or main question) is pending, you can do so after an amendment has been acted on and the main motion, as amended, is before the assembly.

The motion to Postpone [a matter] Indefinitely opens the motion to be postponed to debate just as if that original motion were itself before the assembly. For that reason, though, you may need to call for the Previous Question (Section 20) to cut off debate and bring the matter to a vote.

To Lay on the Table. The motion to table something is commonly used to suppress a question. However, a two-thirds vote should be required to stop debate and suppress a matter (see Section 39).

Suppose that there would be no chance of getting a majority vote during the rest of the current session to take up a matter later. In that case, if you knew it wouldn't be taken up later in the session, a sure way of suppressing the matter would be to get a motion passed to Lay [it] on the Table (Section 19). Since you can't debate a motion to table something, the majority could immediately put the matter aside and be certain that it wouldn't be taken up again without majority consent.

Because of this motion's high rank (see Precedence of Motions list in the Quick-Reference Guide) and the fact that it can't be debated, it is commonly used to suppress a question. On the other hand, its effect is merely to put a matter aside until the assembly decides to consider it (see Section 57). It suppresses something, therefore, only as long as a majority remains opposed to taking it up.

Section 60. To Consider a Question a Second Time

To Reconsider. There's only one way to consider a matter a second time during the same session after it already has been adopted, rejected, or suppressed: You can move to Reconsider (Section 27) the vote on it. However, to make the motion to Reconsider it, you must have voted on the prevailing side (either for or against) when the question was first considered.

A motion to Reconsider the original vote has to be made on the day the vote was taken or on the next succeeding day. (In Congress, if "yeas and nays" [see Section 38] are not taken on a vote, anyone can move to Reconsider it. But yeas and nays are ordered on all important votes in Congress, something that isn't the case in ordinary groups.)

The motion to Reconsider a vote can be made and recorded in the minutes in the middle of debate even when someone has the floor (but it won't be acted on until later). The motion also can be made while another question is pending, although it can't be considered until there is no longer any other matter before the assembly. At that time, if the motion to Reconsider a vote, which was made earlier, is called up, it takes precedence over every other motion except to Adjourn (Section 11) and to Fix the Time to Which to Adjourn (Section 10).

If you make a motion to Reconsider a vote, on a debatable question, it will open to debate the entire merits of the original (debatable) question. But if the original matter is undebatable, the reconsideration of the vote on it also will be undebatable. Whether or not a motion to Reconsider a vote on something opens the original subject to debate, therefore, depends on whether or not that original subject was debatable.

If a motion to Reconsider a vote carries, the chair will state that the question is again on adopting the original matter. This means that the original matter is now treated as though no vote had ever been taken on it, and it, therefore, has to be voted on again before it can be disposed of.

Assume that you made a motion to Reconsider a vote on something on the same day the original vote was taken and that your motion was therefore allowed and recorded in the minutes. But other business may have been before the assembly, so it couldn't be acted on immediately. Depending on the rules of your organization, you may not have to call it up that same day as long as you make the motion to Reconsider on that day. You may be able to wait to call it up until the next meeting *on a succeeding day*.

Waiting to call up the matter on a succeeding day may not be allowed if your organization has no rule to allow it. In that case, if your motion to Reconsider isn't acted on before the close of the session when the original question was adopted, the motion will be lost.

Another possibility is that you decide not to, or are unable to, call up the motion to Reconsider the matter the same day as the original vote or even the next day. If you don't do it then, someone else may call it up that day. If there's no succeeding meeting (adjourned or regular) within, say, a month, however, and no one else calls up the matter on the day you move to Reconsider it, the effect of your motion will end with the adjournment of the meeting at which you make the motion.

The only way to consider a subject a second time, then, within the same session is to move to Reconsider the vote on the original question. This doesn't apply to a motion to Adjourn, although a motion to Adjourn can be *renewed* if business or debate has progressed; the vote on adjournment can't be reconsidered, however.

This rule about reconsideration doesn't prevent an assembly from *renewing* (see Section 26) any of the motions mentioned in Section 7 (subsidiary or secondary motions), if a question before the assembly has changed. In that case, although the motions may be basically the same ones, they are nevertheless technically different.

> *Example:* To move to postpone a resolution is different from moving to postpone it after it has been amended, so the question now, being different as a result of the amendment, can be taken up again. A motion to Suspend the Rules (Section 18), though, can't be renewed at the same meeting, although it can be taken up again at an adjourned (continued) meeting. If a call for Orders of the Day (Section 13) is voted down, it can't be renewed while a matter before the assembly is still under consideration. (See Section 27 for many unusual aspects of this motion and Section 25 concerning the motion to Rescind.)

Section 61. Orders and Rules

Call for Orders of the Day. Sometimes an assembly decides that certain matters should be considered at a particular time. When that time comes, then, those matters are known as Orders of the Day (Section 13). If you were to call for the Orders of the Day, your motion would need no second, so the chair could immediately put your motion to a vote:

> **Will the assembly proceed now to the Orders of the Day?**
>
> **Shall we return to our original schedule?**

If the vote is yes, whatever subject is being considered must be put aside, and the subjects that are supposed to be considered at that time are taken up in their assigned order. The chair, in fact, may not even wait for someone to make a motion but may simply announce a return to the Orders of the Day without any vote, if no one objects. But if someone makes a motion to return to the scheduled order of business and it fails, the motion can't be renewed until the subject presently being considered is first disposed of. (See Section 13 for a fuller explanation.)

Call for Special Orders. Sometimes a subject is so important that it's best to consider it at a special time even in preference to the Orders of the Day and any regularly established order of business. You could then move to make the subject a Special Order (Section 13) for that particular time. To be adopted, your motion would need a two-thirds vote, because it's really a suspension of the rules. Such a motion would be in order, therefore, whenever a motion to Suspend the Rules would be in order.

If a subject is made a Special Order for a particular day, on that day it supersedes all other business except for the reading of the minutes. A Special Order can be postponed, though, by a majority vote. Also, if two Special Orders are made for the same day, the one made first takes precedence over the next one.

To Suspend the Rules. Every assembly that allows discussion needs rules to avoid a lot of wasted time and to help it accomplish its reason for meeting. Nevertheless, it's sometimes necessary to suspend the rules *temporar-*

ily. To do this you can make a motion to Suspend the Rules (Section 18) that interfere with so and so.

If a motion to Suspend the Rules is carried by a two-thirds vote, you can then proceed with whatever you want to accomplish. But a vote isn't always necessary. By general consent (if no one objects), the rules can be temporarily ignored at any time without the formality of a motion and a two-thirds vote.

Questions of Order. The chair has to enforce the rules and preserve order. When you notice a breach of order, you can ask to have the rules enforced. First, address the chair:

Madam Chairman, I rise to a point of order.

Point of order.

The chair will then ask whoever is speaking to sit down and will listen to your comments. Having heard the point of order, the chair will make a decision and may let the person who was speaking continue—with a reminder to stop doing whatever was ruled to be out of order. But when a speaker has violated the rules of proper behavior, he or she may not continue if anyone objects without first getting the permission of the assembly through an affirmative vote.

If someone is using improper language, you might simply state:

I call the speaker to order.

In that case, the chair, again, would decide if the language really is disorderly before letting the speaker continue.

To Appeal. Although the chair decides matters of order, interpretation of the rules, and priority of business, anyone can "appeal from the decision" of the chair. If you move to Appeal (Section 14) the chair's decision on a matter and your motion is seconded, the chair will first state again his or her decision and note the fact that it was "appealed from." Then the chair will state the resulting motion:

Shall the decision of the chair be sustained?

Without leaving his or her seat, the chair can then give reasons for the decision and open the matter to debate (no one may speak more than once), unless the decision is undebatable, as in these cases:

- When it pertains to a violation of the rules of speaking, to some improper behavior, or to the priority of business

- When a motion calling for the Previous Question (Section 20) is pending at the time the Question of Order is raised

After a vote is taken on an appeal, the chair should state that the decision of the chair is sustained or reversed, as the case may be.

Section 62. Miscellaneous

Reading of Papers and Withdrawal of a Motion. Suppose that you want to read a paper (see Section 16) or move to Withdraw a Motion (Section 17) that you made after it was stated by the chair. If anyone objects, it's necessary to make another motion requesting that the assembly grant you permission.

Question of Privilege. Assume that a disturbance occurs in a meeting or something else happens that affects the rights of the assembly or any of its members. You can then rise to a Question of Privilege (Section 12) and state the matter. After hearing your comments, the chair will decide whether it really is a matter of privilege. As usual, members can appeal the chair's decision.

If the matter really is one of privilege, it supersedes, for the time being, the business before the assembly. There are several steps the assembly can take, however, to affect that status. You could make the following motions:

- To Postpone to a Certain Time (Section 21) the Question of Privilege

- To call for the Previous Question (Section 20), which would stop debate and bring the Question of Privilege to a vote

- To Lay [the Question of Privilege] on the Table (Section 19)

- To Refer (Section 22) the Question of Privilege to a committee, which would examine it and report on it.

In any case, as soon as the Question of Privilege is disposed of, the debate that was previously in progress resumes.

Section 63. To Close a Meeting

To Fix the Time to Which to Adjourn. When you want to have an adjourned (continued) meeting of an assembly, make a motion to set the time before it closes:

> **I move that when this assembly adjourns, it adjourn to meet at ＿＿＿ time.**

You can amend such a motion by changing the time. But if you make the motion when another motion is before the assembly, neither the motion for adjournment to a particular time nor the amendment can be debated. On the other hand, if you make the motion when nothing else is before the assembly, it stands the same as any other main motion and thus can be debated.

You can make a motion to Fix the Time to Which to Adjourn (Section 10) even while the assembly is voting on a motion simply to Adjourn (Section 11) (without day). But you cannot make that motion when someone else has the floor.

To Adjourn. An assembly might be kept in session an unreasonably long time if an organization didn't have a rule to limit the time each person could have the floor. (Ten minutes are allowed by Robert's rules of order.)

When you want to end a meeting, then, you either have to wait for someone speaking to yield the floor or have to wait until the person's time is up.

As soon as the floor is available, you should move to Adjourn (Section 11). After there's a second, the chair will immediately put your motion to a vote, since no amendment or debate is allowed. If the vote is affirmative, the chair will state:

> **The motion is carried; this assembly stands adjourned.**

If no other meeting is forthcoming, the chair should state:

> **The motion is carried; this assembly stands adjourned without day [*sine die*].**

If earlier it was decided that the assembly would adjourn to meet at a particular time, the chair would state:

> **The motion is carried; this assembly stands adjourned until [*time*].**

Suppose that you want to qualify a motion to Adjourn by stating a time (to adjourn to tomorrow evening). In that case, you must wait if another matter is before the assembly since a motion stating the time, like any other main motion, can be amended and debated. (See Section 11 for the effect of an adjournment on unfinished business.)

Article XIII. Miscellaneous

Section 64. Debate

In debate, you should always direct your remarks to the chair, stick to the question before the assembly, and avoid any focus on personalities or comments about someone else's motives. Permanent organizations usually adopt rules limiting the number of times any person may speak on the same question and how long the speech may be. If there weren't some time limits in debate, a person could defeat a measure by prolonging his or her speech and by refusing to yield the floor (except for a motion to Adjourn).

In ordinary groups, each member should be allowed two speeches (except on an Appeal [Section 14]). Robert's rules also limit the time to ten minutes per speech. A member may speak more often or longer if the assembly gives him or her permission by a two-thirds vote. The motion requesting such permission can't be debated. (The House allows one speech of one hour per member. The Senate allows two speeches of any length per person.)

Suppose that an assembly wants even more freedom in debate on a matter. It could then consider the matter informally or turn itself into a committee of the whole (see Sections 32 and 33). Or an assembly might want greater limits. In that case, debate could be restricted more or even stopped completely by a two-thirds vote (see Section 58).

Section 65. Form of Stating and Putting Questions

When a motion is made and seconded, assuming the motion is in order, the chair will state the motion to the assembly. A second to a motion is required when it's necessary to ensure that a person introducing something isn't the only one in favor of it. In other cases, such as routine matters or those that clearly are supported by many, a second is usually not needed, and the chair just assumes that the motion is "seconded."

In routine matters, the chair often puts something to a vote without even waiting for a formal motion. Few people like to make formal motions on simple, routine matters, and a lot of time would be wasted waiting for them. But the chair can proceed without a motion only if no one objects.

A presiding officer also can save time by not taking a vote on a routine matter. The chair, therefore, might announce that if there's no objection, so and so will be considered the action of the assembly. After a treasurer's report, for instance, the chair might state:

> **If there's no objection, the report will be referred to an auditing committee consisting of Ms. Webster and Mr. Lopez. [*Pause to see if anyone objects.*] It is so referred.**

These motions do not have to be seconded:

- Call for Orders of the Day (Section 13)
- Questions of Order (Section 14)
- Objection to Consideration of a Question (Section 15)

Common forms of stating a motion are as follows:

> **It has been moved and seconded that [*motion*].**
>
> **The question is on [*subject*].**

With resolutions, one might state (after they were read):

> **The question is on the adoption of the resolutions just read.**

Sometimes, to be very clear, the chair should not merely repeat the motion but should also state that the question is on its adoption. With an Appeal, the chair would first state the chair's decision (and, if appropriate, the reasons for it), next state that the decision has been appealed from, and then state the question:

> **The question is, shall the decision of the chair be sustained?**

In putting the motion to a vote, the chair would add:

> **Those in favor of sustaining the decision of the chair say aye. [*Pause for vote.*] Those opposed say no.**

If the ayes have it, the chair should announce the result:

**The ayes have it, and the decision of the chair
is sustained.**

The decision of the chair is sustained.

In stating a motion for an amendment, the chair should
first read:

• The passage to be amended

• The words to be struck out, if any

• The words to be inserted, if any

• The whole passage as it will stand if the amendment
is adopted

After that, the chair would state the question:

**The question is, shall the word *censure* be in-
serted in the resolution in place of the word
thanks?**

As soon as a vote is taken, the chair should immediately
state the question (if any) that is again before the assembly. In other words, if the assembly has just voted on an
amendment, the chair would announce the result and
then state:

**The question is again on the resolution [*or* "on
the resolution as amended"].**

If an amendment is reconsidered, the chair should announce the result of the vote and state the question before the assembly in a form such as this:

**The motion is carried—the vote on the amend-
ment is reconsidered. The question is again on
the adoption of the amendment. [*See Section
31 about acting on committee reports and on
papers with several paragraphs.*]**

After stating the question on a matter that can be amended or debated, the chair should pause to see if anyone immediately rises or speaks and, if not, ask:

Are you ready for the question?

The following forms are common in some groups:

Are there any remarks [*or* "further remarks"]?

Is there any further discussion?

When the chair believes the debate is closed, he or she would again ask:

Are you ready for the question?

If no one rises or speaks this time, the chair will state the motion once more and immediately put it to a vote. A common form of putting a question to a vote (after it has been stated again) is this:

Those in favor of the motion say aye [*or* "hold up their right hands"]. [*Pause for vote.*] Those opposed say no [*or, again,* "hold up their right hands"].

See Sections 38, 46–48, and 54 for examples of various ways to state motions and put them to a vote. See the Quick-Reference Guide for unusual forms.

PART III.
MISCELLANEOUS

Article XIV. Legal Rights

Section 66. Right of Deliberative Assemblies to Punish Members

A deliberative assembly has a right to make and enforce its own laws and punish offenders. The most extreme penalty it may impose is expelling a member. If the assembly is a permanent organization, it may (to the extent required for its own protection) give public notice that the offender is no longer a member of its organization.

But an organization may not go beyond what's necessary for self-protection. It may not, for example, publish the charges against an expelled member. In one such case, an officer of a society published—on order of the society—a statement of the serious charges of which a member had been found guilty. The expelled member then brought a libel suit against the officer and recovered damages after the court had ruled that the society erred and that it didn't matter whether the charges were true.

Section 67. Right of an Assembly to Eject Someone from a Meeting

A deliberative assembly has the right to decide who may be present during a session. When an assembly decides by rule or vote that someone may not remain in the room, the chair has to enforce that rule or order (with or without police or legal assistance, as deemed prudent).

When someone must be taken out of a meeting, the chair may decide to direct other members to escort the person out, without calling the police. The members doing this, however, should be careful not to use harsher treatment than is necessary. (The courts have held previously that anyone who is unnecessarily harsh is liable to prosecution the same as any member of the police force would be under the same circumstances.) But usually, neither the chair nor the organization itself will be liable for damages. They merely ordered the member's removal, which does not exceed their legal rights.

Section 68. Rights of Ecclesiastical Tribunals

Many deliberative assemblies are ecclesiastical bodies, and it's important to know to what extent civil courts will respect their decisions. One interesting case went to the U.S. Supreme Court.

> *Example:* A church became divided, and each party claimed to be the church; each one, therefore, also claimed to be entitled to the church property. The case first went to the civil courts and, finally, on appeal, to the Supreme Court. The Court held it under advisement for a year before reversing the decision of the state court. That decision was based on the fact that the state court ruling conflicted with a decision of the highest ecclesiastical court that had acted on the case.
>
> In its decision, the Supreme Court laid down this broad principle: When a local church is only part of a large and more general organization or denomination, the court will accept as final the decision of the highest ecclesiastical tribunal to which the case had been carried within that general church organization. It won't inquire into the justice or injustice of its decree in regard to the parties before it. The officers, ministers, members, or church body that are recognized by the highest judiciary of the denomination will also be recognized by the

court. When the church body expels or cuts off any members, therefore, the court also will hold that they're no longer members of that church.

Section 69. Trial of Members of Societies

Since a deliberative assembly has the right to expel someone, it also has to have the right to investigate the character of its members. It can require that any member must testify in a case or, upon refusal to do so, may be expelled.

Charges against a member's character are usually referred to a committee of investigation or discipline or to some standing committee. The committee then has to report its findings to the organization. Some organizations have standing committees formed to report any disciplinary cases that arise.

In matters of discipline, a committee's report to the organization doesn't have to go into detail but should give recommendations for action that the organization should take. It usually would close with resolutions covering the case, so there shouldn't be any need for someone else to offer additional resolutions. When the recommendation is expulsion, the ordinary resolutions are as follows:

- To fix the Time to Which to Adjourn (Section 10)

- To instruct the secretary, or clerk, to cite the member to appear before the organization at the adjourned (continued) meeting, where the member must show cause why he or she should not be expelled in view of the charges

- To list the charges against the member

After charges have been brought against a member and an assembly has ordered that the person be cited to appear for "trial," the member is theoretically "under arrest." He or she is deprived of all rights of membership until the case is resolved. Without a member's consent, though, the individual shouldn't be tried at the same meeting at which the charges were preferred unless the charges relate to something done specifically at that meeting.

It's the secretary's duty to send the accused person a written notice to appear before the organization at the appointed time. At the same time, the secretary should give the accused individual a copy of the charges. If the accused person doesn't obey the summons, the organization usually considers that act cause enough for summary expulsion.

The trial takes place at the appointed meeting. Often the only evidence required is the committee report. The committee chair or someone else from the committee then reads the report and offers any additional evidence that the committee wants to introduce.

After that, the accused person should be allowed to give an explanation and introduce witnesses. Each party should be allowed to cross-examine the other's witnesses and introduce rebutting testimony.

As soon as all evidence is in, the accused should leave the room, and the organization should consider the matter. Finally, the organization should vote on the question of expulsion or any other proposed punishment. No one should be expelled, however, by less than a two-thirds vote, with a quorum required for voting. (The U.S. Constitution [Article 1, Section 5] provides that each house of Congress may, "with the concurrence of two-thirds, expel a member.")

There's a vast distinction between the evidence needed to convict someone in a civil court and that required to convict an accused person in an ordinary organization or an ecclesiastical body. A notorious pickpocket, for instance, couldn't even be arrested let alone convicted in a civil court simply because he or she was known as a pickpocket. But that would be enough "evidence" for an ordinary organization to convict and expel someone. Moral belief in the truth of some charges against a member may be all that an ecclesiastical or other deliberative body needs to find a person guilty of charges.

If a trial is likely to be long and troublesome or very delicate, the accused person is often cited to appear before a committee instead of the entire organization. The committee would then report the results of its trial of the case. This would include resolutions covering the punishment it recommends that the organization adopt.

After the committee report has been read to the entire organization, the accused person should be allowed to make a statement, and the committee should be allowed to reply. When that's over, the accused individual should leave the room so that the organization can act on the committee's resolutions. Committee members would vote on the case the same as the other members.

An accused person might ask to be represented by counsel at the trial. If so, an organization would usually allow this, although the counsel should be a member of the organization in good standing. But if the counsel is guilty of improper conduct during the trial, the organization could refuse to hear any more and could also punish that person (as a member).

Section 70. Call of the House

A *call of the house* is an order that compels absent members to attend a meeting. But it's a process that's allowed only in assemblies that have a rule providing this power. (A call doesn't apply in voluntary organizations.) Usually, when no quorum is present, a small number (one-fifth of the members-elect in Congress) can order a call of the house.

In the early history of Congress, a call of the house required a day's notice. In the English Parliament, it's customary to order a call for a certain future date, usually not over ten days later, although it has been as long as six weeks later. The object is to give notice so that all members may be present on that day when important business is scheduled to come up. In Congress, a call nowadays is used only when no quorum is present. As soon as a quorum appears, further proceedings in the call (see the explanation later in this section under *"Proceedings in a Call of the House"*) are usually

> dispensed with, and this is in order at any stage of
> the proceedings. In some legislative bodies, though,
> proceedings in the call can't be ignored unless a
> majority of the members-elect vote to do so. In
> Congress, it's customary after the call to pay the
> fees that were assessed for being absent.

To prevent an assembly from using a call improperly,
it's a good idea to provide that when the call is made,
the members can't adjourn or dispense with further proceedings in the call until a quorum is obtained. A rule
such as that in the following example would work in
city councils and similar bodies that have the power to
enforce attendance:

> *Example:* **When no quorum is present, members
> may order a call of the house and compel the
> attendance of absent members. After the call is
> ordered, a motion to adjourn or dispense with
> further proceedings in the call cannot be enter-
> tained until a quorum is present or until the
> sergeant-at-arms reports that in his or her opin-
> ion no quorum can be obtained that day.**

If a quorum isn't present, a call of the house takes
precedence over everything, even the reading of the minutes, except for the motion to Adjourn (Section 11). To
take effect, a call requires an affirmative vote for it by
the number specified in the organization's rule (one-fifth,
for example). If the rule allows for a motion making a
call while a quorum is present (for the purpose of getting
a larger attendance), the call should rank with Questions
of Privilege (see Section 12) and require a majority vote
to be adopted. If a call is rejected, it shouldn't be made
again while a quorum is present at that meeting (see
Section 42).

After a call is ordered and until further proceedings
in the call are dispensed with, no motion is in order
except one to Adjourn or another motion relating to
the call. A recess, then, couldn't be taken by unanimous
consent. An adjournment ends all proceedings in the

call, although before the adjournment, if a quorum is present, the assembly can order "arrested" members to make their excuses at an adjourned meeting.

Proceedings in a Call of the House. When the call is ordered, the secretary calls the roll alphabetically and notes which members are absent. The secretary then calls the names of just the absentees, at which time explanations of absence can be requested. (Congress usually excuses members who have "paired off," which refers to two members on opposite sides of a pending question who have both agreed to stay away. But the absence of both members must not affect the result, which would rarely happen in municipal bodies.)

After the roll call and the excuses, the doors are locked, and no one may leave. An order similar to the following is adopted:

> **That the sergeant-at-arms take into custody and bring to the bar of the House such of its members as are absent without leave of the House.**

A warrant is signed by the presiding officer and attested by the secretary with a list of absentees attached. This is given to the sergeant-at-arms, who immediately "arrests" the absent members.

According to House Rule 22: "It shall be the duty of the Sergeant-at-Arms to attend the House during its sittings; to aid in the enforcement of orders, under the direction of the Speaker; to execute the commands of the House from time to time; together with all such process, issued by authority thereof, as shall be directed to him by the Speaker." The words *sergeant-at-arms* can be replaced in the order by *chief of police* or whatever officer is designated to serve the process.

The sergeant-at-arms then appears with various members "under arrest"; goes to the chair's desk (after being announced by the doorkeeper in large bodies), followed by the "arrested" members; and returns to his or her post.

The chair "arraigns" each member separately and asks what excuse each has for being absent from the assembly without leave. Each member gives an excuse, and someone moves that the person be released from custody and allowed to take a seat either without paying a fee or after paying the required fine. But until a member has paid any fees assessed for the absence, he or she can't vote or be recognized by the chair for any purpose.

Quick-Reference
Guide to Motions

A large part of meeting conduct concerns *motions*—statements that participants make to introduce business or to propose something requiring a decision, or vote. Dictionaries commonly describe *motions* as formal proposals for acting, especially when made in a deliberative assembly. For a decision to be reached, then, someone has to "make a motion" proposing it.

Since this activity is predominant in most meetings, the 1893 *Robert's Rules of Order* appropriately provided a quick-reference table of rules about motions, similar to the one given here. According to General Robert, this table capsules data that will enable you "to decide some two hundred questions of parliamentary law without turning a page." The table provides the following information:

- An index to the various sections in the book that discuss each motion in detail (Refer to the section numbers along the left column of the table where the motions are listed alphabetically.)

- A classification of the various motions according to whether they (1) are debatable, (2) open main motions to debate, (3) cannot be amended, (4) cannot be reconsidered, (5) require a two-thirds vote, (6) do not need to be seconded, (7) are in order when another person has the floor (Refer to the asterisks [*] in the seven columns of the table to see which rules, if any, apply to each motion.)

- A determination of the motions to which the above seven categories apply *in part* (Refer to the notes to the table and the corresponding note numbers in each of the seven columns.)

Two additional lists follow this table:

1. Precedence of Motions (which ones are more important and must be decided first) and whether they can be amended or debated and what vote they require to pass (such as a two-thirds vote)

2. Forms of Putting Certain Questions (the correct formal wording to use to state a motion and ask for a vote on it)

How to Use the Table During a Meeting

When you're in the middle of a meeting, you don't have time to start reading a book of rules or to page through such a book to hunt for various sections. The following tables and lists are meant to provide fast answers. For example, assume that you're conducting a meeting and someone makes a motion while another motion is pending. Glance at the Precedence of Motions list (page 256) to see if the second motion is in order. (A lower-rank motion, for example, can't supersede one of a higher order.) Then look for the motion in the left column of the Rules about Motions table. Check the adjacent seven columns in the table for asterisks and footnote numbers. If there are no asterisks in the columns, you know that:

- The motion is debatable.

- The debate must be strictly confined to the motion.

- The motion can be amended.

- The motion can be reconsidered.

- The motion must have a majority vote to be adopted.

- The motion must be seconded.

- The motion is not in order when another person has the floor.

An asterisk in one of the columns, however, means that the motion is an exception to the general rule. A note number in the column refers to one of the notes to the table that explains to what extent it is an exception.

> *Example:* Imagine that you're conducting a meeting and that an amendment of a resolution is before the assembly when someone makes a motion ("moves") to Refer it to a committee ("to Commit"). First check the Precedence of Motions list, where you will find that "to Commit" is in order—it stands above "to Amend." Next, check the table of rules, where you will discover that the motion differs from an ordinary resolution because it "opens to debate the main question" (the original resolution). If someone then moves to "Postpone [the question] Indefinitely," you should rule it out of order according to the Precedence of Motions list (it's of *lower* rank than "to Commit"). On the other hand, if someone moves "to Lay [the question] on the Table," you would find that it takes precedence over "to Commit" and is in order (it's of *higher* rank). The table of rules would then immediately clarify the seven pertinent points (or rules) for you. (To learn more about how to find such information in the table, refer to the Explanation at the top of the table.)

By checking the lists and the table (including notes and the introductory Explanation) you can quickly decide how to handle motions as they're made in a meeting. Eventually, if you conduct many formal meetings, you'll no doubt want to memorize the rules about the most common motions. But for the others, a quick-reference table is indispensable. However, don't rely on the table alone. Before you conduct a formal meeting, *read the text of this book* describing the rules of order and the organization and conduct of business. Those text sections will help you to become familiar with terminology such as "lay the question on the table," to learn what the duties of the various officers and committees are, and to become adept at managing debates and other meeting activities.

Precedence of Motions

The following list shows the rank of common motions. any motion (except to Amend) can be made while another *lower*-rank motion is pending. But no motion can supersede another motion of *higher* rank. The motion calling for the Previous Question requires a two-thirds vote; all others need only a majority.

Motions	Can Be Amended	Cannot Be Amended
Undebatable Motions		
To Fix the Time to Which to Adjourn (*when another question is before the assembly*)	X	
To Adjourn (*when unqualified*)		X
To call for the Orders of the Day		X
To Lay on the Table		X
To call for the Previous Question (*requires two-thirds vote*)		X
Debatable Motions		
To Postpone to a Certain Time	X	
To Commit or Refer	X	
To Amend	X	
To Postpone Indefinitely		X

The motion to Reconsider can be made when any other question is before the assembly. But it can't be acted on until the other question is disposed of (see note 9 to table) when, if it's called up, it takes precedence over all other motions (except to Adjourn and to Fix the Time to Which to Adjourn). Questions that are incidental to those before the assembly take precedence over them and must be acted on first.

Forms of Putting Certain Questions

"Putting a question" is parliamentary terminmology for placing a motion before an assembly for a vote. Various sections in the text describe common formal and informal forms for stating a motion and putting it to a vote. The following are examples of unusual forms:

- To demand or call for the Previous Question is to move that debate cease and the assembly vote on the pending question(s). The chair might ask: "Shall we stop debate and have an immediate vote on the pending question [*or* 'resolution' *or* 'amendment']?" (See Section 20.)

- To Appeal from the decision of the chair is to object to a decision made by the chair. The chair might ask: "Shall the decision of the chair be sustained?" (See Section 14.)

- To call for the Orders of the Day is to ask to have the assembly conform to its designated schedule or order of business. If the chair fails to announce business in the proper order and orders are called for, the chair might ask: "Is the assembly in favor of returning to the schedule?" (See Section 13.)

- When a question is introduced and someone voices an Objection to Consideration of the Question, the chair might ask: "Will the assembly sustain the objection?" (See Section 15.)

- Voting may be by ballot, show of hands, roll call,

Rules About Motions

Explanation: The left column of the table lists the various motions alphabetically and gives the number of the accompanying section in the text discussing the motions. The seven column headings are the main rules that apply to motions. An asterisk [*] in one of the seven columns means that the rule described in the column head applies to the adjacent motion in the left column. A note number means that the rule only partially applies, and the extent to which it applies is described in the note itself. For example, "Lay on the Table" is a motion discussed in Section 19 of the text. Asterisks in two columns show that it's undebatable and can't be amended. Note 5 indicates that an affirmative vote on this motion can't be reconsidered. The other four columns are blank, meaning that the motion does *not* "open the main question to debate," does *not* "require a two-thirds vote," *does* "need to be seconded," and is *not* "in order when another member has the floor."

Section	Motion	In order when another has the floor (§2)	Does not require to be seconded (§3)	Requires a two-thirds vote (§39). See n.l.	Cannot be reconsidered (§27)	Cannot be amended (§23)	Opens main question to debate (§35)	Undebatable (§35)
11	Adjourn				*	*		*
10	Adjourn, Fix the Time to Which to							2
23	Amend (n.3)							
23	Amend an Amendment					*		
45	Amend the Rules			*				
14	Appeal, relating to indecorum etc. (n.4)					*		*

Notes

1. Every motion in this column has the effect of suspending some rule or established right of deliberative assemblies (see Section 39) and, therefore, requires a two-thirds vote, unless a special rule to the contrary is adopted.

2. Undebatable if made when another question is before the assembly.

3. An amendment may be made either (a) by adding or (b) by striking out words or (c) by striking out certain words and inserting others or (d) by substituting a different motion on the same subject or (e) by dividing the question into two or more questions as specified by the mover so as to get a separate vote on any particular point(s).

4. An appeal is undebatable only when relating to indecorum (see Section 36) or to transgressions of the rules of speaking (see Sections 34, 36, 64) or to the priority of business or when made while the Previous Question is pending. When an Appeal is debatable,

Ref	Motion								Notes
14	Appeal, all other cases		*	*			*	*	only one speech from each member is permitted. On a tie vote the decision of the chair is sustained.
14	Call to Order		*	*				*	
37	Close Debate, motion to							*	5. An affirmative vote on this motion can't be reconsidered.
22	Commit or Refer	*						2	
34	Extend the Limits of Debate, motion to					*		*	
10	Fix the Time to Which to Adjourn			*				*	
36	Leave to Continue Speaking after Indecorum		5					*	6. The objection can be made only when the question is first introduced, before debate.
19	Lay on the Table							*	
37	Limit Debate, motion to			*			*	*	
15	Objection to Consideration of a Question (n.6)			*		*	*	*	7. Allows only limited debate on the propriety of the postponement.
13	Orders of the Day, motion for the					*	*	7	
21	Postpone to a Certain Time		*					*	
24	Postpone Indefinitely		*	*		*		*	8. The Previous Question, if adopted, cuts off debate and brings the assembly to a vote on the pending question only, except where the pending motion is an amendment or a motion to Commit, when it also applies to the question to be amended or committed.
20	Previous Question (n.8)		*	*				*	
44	Priority of Business, questions relating to		*					*	
12	Privilege, Questions of			*				*	
16	Reading Papers		*					*	
27	Reconsider a Debatable Question	*	*		9			*	
27	Reconsider an Undebatable Questions	*	*		9			*	
22	Refer (same as Commit)							*	
25	Rescind							*	
11	Rise (in Committee: Adjourn)		*					*	9. Can be moved and entered on the record when another person has the floor but can't interrupt business then before the assembly; must be made on the day or the day after the original vote was taken and by one who voted with the prevailing side.
13	Special Order, to make a				*			*	
23	Substitute (same as Amend, n.3)			*	5			*	
18	Suspend the Rules							*	
19	Take from the Table				5			*	
44	Take up a Question Out of Its Proper Order							*	
17	Withdrawal of a Motion							*	

general consent, or voice. If the vote is ordered to be taken by "yeas and nays" (by voice; see Section 38), the chair might state: "Those in favor of adopting these resolutions will, when their names are called, answer yes [*or* 'aye']. Those opposed will answer no." (See Section 38.)

INDEX